C000002499

BRADSHAW'S
HISTORY

Vic Bradshaw-Mitchell

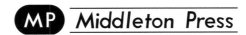

Front cover: The House of Bradshaw was the term used for the offices of Bradshaw and Blacklock at 27, Brown-Street, Manchester.

Back cover: George Bradshaw: a rare portrait. His grave in Oslo is maintained by the local authority. The city was called Christiania when he died and until 1925.

Published April 2012

ISBN 978 1 908174 18 5

© Middleton Press, 2012

Design Emma Esher

Published by
    Middleton Press
    Easebourne Lane
    Midhurst
    West Sussex
    GU29 9AZ
Tel: 01730 813169
Fax: 01730 812601
Email: info@middletonpress.co.uk
www.middletonpress.co.uk

Printed in the United Kingdom by Henry Ling Limited, at the Dorset Press, Dorchester, DT1 1HD

CONTENTS

INTRODUCTION

The story begins in the early 19th century with the young George Bradshaw perfecting his skills as a cartographer, in the canal era. This he extended to railways as they began to expand and railway timetables were added to his output from 1839.

Told herein is how he created a massive business with the help of others and how it became international. His early death in Norway did not stop the product range growing. Its demise in the 1960s is chronicled.

The story of the revival of the Bradshaw name in the early 21st century is outlined, this culminating in around 20 references per hour in the BBC TV series *Great British Railway Journeys*, which Mr Portillo began introducing in 2009.

The first five chapters date from 1939 and were written for the centenary of Bradshaw's first timetable. The remainder tell the subsequent story of the famous name.

CHAPTER I

IN THE BEGINNING

On the 21st May, 1801, at the very threshold of the nineteenth century, His Majesty King George III gave his Royal Assent to an Act authorising the construction of the first Railway in the world definitely empowered by Parliament to throw itself open to the public, and two months later George Bradshaw was born. The Age of Improvement had set in—there was room for it; the March of Progress had begun, and though it was a slow march it was not so slow as the progress made during the preceding century.

A hundred years earlier an advertisement had appeared which read:

York Four Days—Stage Coach.

Begins on Friday the 12th of April, 1706.

All that are desirous to pass from London to York, or from York to London, or any other place on that Road; let them Repair to the Black Swan in Holbourn in London, and to the Black Swan in Coney Street in York;

At both which places, they may be received in a Stage Coach every Monday, Wednesday, and Friday, which performs the whole journey in four days (if God permits), and sets forth at Five in the Morning,

And returns from York to Stamford in two days, and from Stamford, by Huntingdon, to London in two days more. And the like Stages on their return;

Allowing each Passenger 14lb. weight, and all above 3d. a Pound.

Performed by { Benjamin Kingman, Henry Harrison, Walter Baynes.

Also this gives Notice, that a Newcastle Stage Coach sets out from York every Monday and Friday, and from Newcastle every Monday and Friday.

Thanks very largely to John Metcalf of the rather long nickname " Blind Jack of Knaresborough;" John Loudon Macadam, who gave a new word to the English language; and Thomas Telford who was embarrassed with the two highly classical aliases " The Colossus of Roads " and " Pontifex Maximus;" such improvements had been made by 1822 that the Proprietors were not only able to perform the journey from London to Stamford in half the time, but started an hour later and made so bold as not to invoke the Almighty's will or the weather's permission.

Their advertisement read:

Six o'clock in the morning from London.

The Proprietors of The Regent Coach Respectfully inform the public and their friends in particular, that, for their more *perfect convenience*, and to keep pace with the daily improvements in *travelling, the hour of its leaving London will be altered* on Monday, the 13th of May (and continued during the summer months),

To six o'clock in the morning
Instead of night.

The arrangements that are forming in furtherance of this long-desired alteration will ensure a steady and punctual conveyance of Passengers to Stamford by a Quarter before Six o'clock and to Melton by a Quarter before Nine o'clock in the evening.

The hours of leaving Melton and Stamford will NOT be altered.

The Proprietors take this opportunity to acknowledge their sense of the decided patronage shewn to the REGENT Coach under their several regulations, and to repeat their promise that no exertion shall be wanting to make it one of the most desirable conveyances to and from London.

Passengers and Parcels booked at Mr. Weldon's, and the Bull and Swan Inn, Stamford; and at Mr. Sharp's, Bell Inn, Melton.—Stamford, May 1st, 1822.

In the meantime the progress of Railways though slow was sure. It had been the boast of James Watt, whose " conversation was at all times rich and instructive in no ordinary degree; and, if possible, still more pleasing than wise," that " the velocity, violence, magnitude, and horrible noise of the engine give universal satisfaction to all beholders ;" and one of the first steam locomotives ever made was chiefly remarkable for having convinced the Vicar of Redruth that he had encountered the personal Devil.

In fact, the infant locomotive needed the genius of Stephenson to redeem it from virtue, and in 1829 the Rocket won a prize of £500 for being the locomotive engine " which shall be a decided improvement on those now in use." That the improvement was decided may be judged from the fact that a year later at the opening of the Liverpool and Manchester Railway the author of *The Fairchild Family* was moved to write that: " The Monsters, being very civil monsters, not only relaxed their energies in passing the stands, but actually backed to give us time to see more of them, for there were several engines, and each had its line of carriages."

Nearly twenty years after, one of Bradshaw's Quaker friends also came under the spell:

> I love to see one of these huge creatures, with sinews of brass and muscles of iron, strut forth from its smoky stable, and saluting the long train of cars with a dozen sonorous puffs from his iron nostrils, fall back gently into his harness. There he stands, champing and foaming upon the iron track, his great heart a furnace of glowing coals; his lymphatic blood is boiling in his veins; the strength of a thousand horses is nerving his sinews; he pants to be gone. He would drag St. Peter's across the desert of the Sahara, if he could be hitched on to it; but there is a little sober-eyed, tobacco-chewing man in the saddle, who holds him in with one finger, and can take away his breath in a moment, should he grow restive or vicious. I am always deeply interested in this man; for, begrimed as he may be with coal, diluted with oil and steam, I regard him as the genius of the whole machinery, as the physical mind of that huge steam horse.

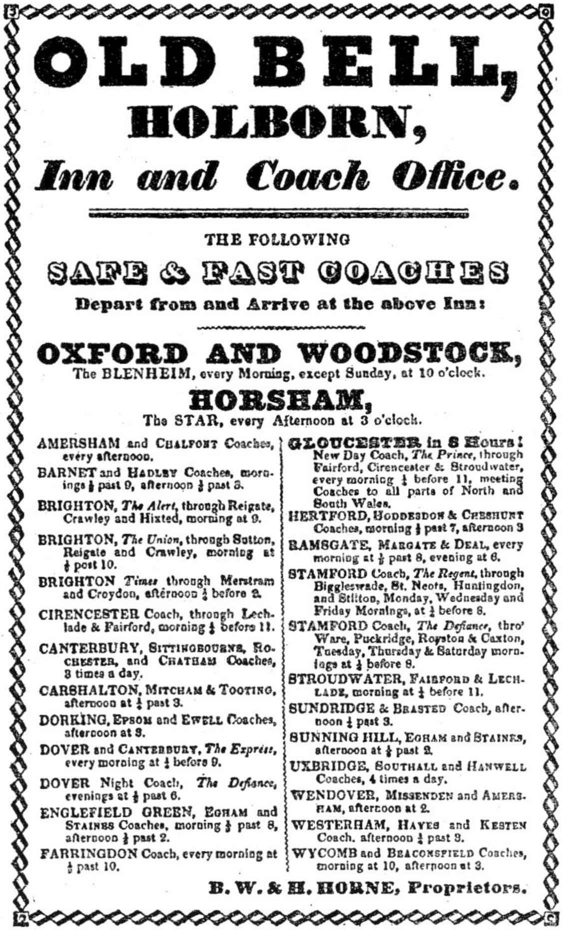

OLD BELL,
HOLBORN,
Inn and Coach Office.

THE FOLLOWING
SAFE & FAST COACHES
Depart from and Arrive at the above Inn:

OXFORD AND WOODSTOCK,
The BLENHEIM, every Morning, except Sunday, at 10 o'clock.

HORSHAM,
The STAR, every Afternoon at 3 o'clock.

AMERSHAM and CHALFONT Coaches, every afternoon.

BARNET and HADLEY Coaches, mornings ½ past 9, afternoon ½ past 3.

BRIGHTON, *The Alert*, through Reigate, Crawley and Hixted, morning at 9.

BRIGHTON, *The Union*, through Sutton, Reigate and Crawley, morning at ½ post 10.

BRIGHTON *Times* through Merstram and Croydon, afternoon ½ before 2.

CIRENCESTER Coach, through Lechlade & Fairford, morning ¼ before 11.

CANTERBURY, SITTINGBOURNE, ROCHESTER, and CHATHAM Coaches, 3 times a day.

CARSHALTON, MITCHAM & TOOTING, afternoon at ½ past 3.

DORKING, EPSOM and EWELL Coaches, afternoon at 3.

DOVER and CANTERBURY, *The Express*, every morning at ½ before 9.

DOVER Night Coach, *The Defiance*, evenings at ½ past 6.

ENGLEFIELD GREEN, EGHAM and STAINES Coaches, morning ½ past 8, afternoon ½ past 2.

FARRINGDON Coach, every morning at ½ past 10.

GLOUCESTER in 8 Hours! New Day Coach, *The Prince*, through Fairford, Cirencester & Stroudwater, every morning ¼ before 11, meeting Coaches to all parts of North and South Wales.

HERTFORD, HODDESDON & CHESHUNT Coaches, morning ½ past 7, afternoon 3

RAMSGATE, MARGATE & DEAL, every morning at ½ past 8, evening at 6.

STAMFORD Coach, *The Regent*, through Biggleswade, St. Neots, Huntingdon, and Stilton, Monday, Wednesday and Friday Mornings, at ½ before 8.

STAMFORD Coach, *The Defiance*, thro' Ware, Puckridge, Royston & Caxton, Tuesday, Thursday & Saturday mornings at ½ before 8.

STROUDWATER, FAIRFORD & LECHLADE, morning at ¼ before 11.

SUNDRIDGE & BRASTED Coach, afternoon ½ past 3.

SUNNING HILL, EGHAM and STAINES, afternoon at ½ past 2.

UXBRIDGE, SOUTHALL and HANWELL Coaches, 4 times a day.

WENDOVER, MISSENDEN and AMERSHAM, afternoon at 2.

WESTERHAM, HAYES and KESTEN Coach, afternoon ½ past 3.

WYCOMB and BEACONSFIELD Coaches, morning at 10, afternoon at 3.

B. W. & H. HORNE, Proprietors.

that the promoters of the Manchester and Leeds Railway, in a " Memorandum for the movers and seconders of Resolutions " at meetings in support of their Bill, arranged for the movers to conclude their speeches with the words:

> We shall, one of these days, hear of a man breakfasting in London, dining in Manchester, supping at Leeds or York, and sleeping in Edinburgh! Then, may the ardent and anxious lover, the object of whose idolatry is in a distant part of the

Kingdom, 'fly on the wings of love,' not in imagination only, but find himself really and corporally in the presence of his mistress, by the potent agency of a railway and locomotive engine, with a rapidity that almost outstrips his ardour; thus realising the poetical extravaganza:

Ye Gods ! annihilate Time and Space,
To make two lovers happy.

At this point, the Promoters, becoming alarmed that a delicate situation might develop, were abashed into a most undramatic anti-climax, for the part of the Second Speaker contained only a few lines:

This is a self-evident proposition . . . . . need not be further enforced . . . . . subject fully and ably treated by preceding speaker.

It was clear The Railway Age was inaugurated, but the general railway Time Table was yet to be evolved by the slow March of Progress.

An old Coaching Bill of that time, 1835, is reproduced opposite, and below a Liverpool and Manchester Railway Time Table, but as early as 1831 the Liverpool and Manchester Railway had published a combination of their Time Tables and those of Coaches running in connection with their trains.

TRAVELLING BY THE
Liverpool and Manchester Railway.
1835.

The following are the Times of Departure both from Liverpool and Manchester.

SEVEN o'Clock	1st Class Train.
Quarter-past Seven o'Clock	2nd Class Train.
TEN o'Clock	1st Class Train.
Half-past Ten o'Clock	2nd Class Train.
Twelve o' Clock	2nd Class Train.
TWO o'Clock	1st Class Train.
Three o'Clock............	2nd Class Train.
FIVE o'Clock..............	1st Class Train.
Half-past Five o'Clock	2nd Class Train.

Except on Tuesdays & Saturdays, when the Evening second class Train from Manchester will start at Six o'Clock, instead of Half-past Five o'Clock; and on Tuesdays and Saturdays, in addition to the above departures, a First Class Train from Manchester will also start at SIX o'Clock in the Evening.

THE FOLLOWING ARE THE DEPARTURES ON SUNDAYS.

Seven o'Clock ,....................	2nd Class Train.
EIGHT o'Clock ....,...........	1st Class Train.
FIVE o'Clock '....................	1st Class Train.
Half-past Five o'Clock	2nd Class Train.

FARES.

By First Class Train, Coaches, Four Inside........	6s.	6d.
,, Ditto, Ditto, Six Inside	5s.	6d.
,, Second Class Train, Glass Coaches	5s.	6d.
,, Ditto, Open Carriages...........	4s.	0d.

Charge for the conveyance of Four-wheeled Carriages 20s. each,
Ditto, Two-wheeled Ditto ...15s. ,,
HORSES—For One Horse 10s.—Two Horses 18s.—Three Horses 22s.

LIVERPOOL AND MANCHESTER
RAILWAY TRAVELLING,

WITH AN

ACCOUNT OF THE TIMES OF DEPARTURE AND ARRIVAL

OF THE

Different Trains, Fares, &c. &c.

ALSO,

LISTS OF THE COACHES

FROM

LIVERPOOL, MANCHESTER, AND CHESTER,

TO VARIOUS PARTS OF THE KINGDOM,

AND OF THE

STEAM PACKETS

FROM

LIVERPOOL TO IRELAND, SCOTLAND, WALES,

AND DIFFERENT PARTS OF THE COAST.

Travellers will keep in view, that the fares by Coaches and Boats, and also the times of departure by them, are frequently varied.

Manchester being about twenty miles nearer to London and most parts of the South than Liverpool, will make that route, in many cases, the most expeditious and cheapest.

The distance (by Liverpool and the Railway) between Chester and Manchester, being only about seven miles more than by the direct road, will be more than compensated, both in time and expense, by the cheapness and expedition of railway travelling.

The best way of passing between Manchester and Southport is through Liverpool.

Manchester and Liverpool being equally distant from Preston and the North, travellers being in either town, and intending to proceed Northward, may go by the Railway, with no other disadvantage than two hours in time, and from three shillings and sixpence to five shillings expense.

PRINTED BY E. SMITH AND CO. LORD-STREET LIVERPOOL.

This was a pamphlet of twelve pages, about 8½in. × 5½ in., and eight of the pages were taken up with particulars of coaches running from Liverpool, Manchester, and Chester. It was planned by Mr. Cropper, a director of the Liverpool and Manchester Railway, who claimed that it was the origin of Bradshaw's Railway Guide. Like Bradshaw, it gave particulars of "Steam Packets from Liverpool," which filled over two pages. Just one-quarter of a page sufficed for the trains on the Liverpool and Manchester Railway.

But the Liverpool and Manchester Railway, like all early railways, was a local institution, and like the railways which immediately followed it, was very much of a novelty. Consequently there appeared a flood of guide books, several for each Railway as it was opened, each containing a history of railways, carefully copied by successive authors, a description of the country through which the particular line passed, and a time table which was possibly obsolete by the date of publication.

Early in 1838 the London and Birmingham Railway was opened from Euston to Denbigh Hall, and from Rugby to Birmingham, and to meet the requirements of passengers there appeared:—

THE

IRON ROAD BOOK

AND

RAILWAY COMPANION

FROM

LONDON

TO

BIRMINGHAM, MANCHESTER,

AND

LIVERPOOL,

CONTAINING AN

Account of the Towns, Villages Mansions, &c.

ON EACH SIDE OF THE LINE;

Times of Arrival and Departure of the Trains

AT THE SEVERAL STATIONS,

Coaches and Omnibuses to the Towns in the Vicinity,

WITH

TABLES OF DISTANCES AND FARES FROM STATION TO STATION

&c. &c.

Illustrated with Maps of the entire Line.

BY FRANCIS COGHLAN,

Author of Guides to 'Paris,' 'St. Petersburgh, ' The Rhine,' ' Belgium, ' Switzerland,' ' London,' &c.

London :

A H. BAILY & Co., 83, CORNHILL.

1838.

The journey from Denbigh Hall to Rugby was performed by Road Coaches, and of the nine coaches that served Denbigh Hall Station, two were named The Railway and one The Rocket. Mr. Coghlan gave the times of the arrival and departure of the trains under each station, and in the Notice at the beginning of the book, dated May 16th, 1838, the author stated that the correctness of the work might be depended upon.

On the 17th September that year, by the opening of the intervening portion between Denbigh Hall and Rugby, through railway communication was established between London, Birmingham, Liverpool, Manchester and Preston, and the time had arrived for the publication of the General Railway Time Table, and Time, as usual, produced the man—George Bradshaw, born at Windsor Bridge, Salford, near Manchester, on July 29th, 1801, two months after the incorporation of the Surrey Iron Railway Company.

3 Distances	Birmingham to London STATIONS.	6 45 a.m. * mixed	7 a.m. mixed	8 30 a.m. §* mail	10 a.m. †‖ mix. call at 1st c.s.	11 a.m. fr. Aylesbury mix.	12 noon *‡‖ mixed	1 15 p.m. *† mix. call at 1st c. st.	2 20 p.m. 3rd class train	4 p.m. ‡‖ mix. call at mail 1st.	4 p.m. *§ 1st class	6 p.m. ‡‖ mixed	12 p.m. *§ mail mixed	1 a.m. ‖‡ From Rugby	Fares. ‡ in car. by day, or 1 cl. 6 in by night	1st cls. car. 6 inside by day	2nd cls. car. closed by night	2d cls. car. open by day
Mls.	Birminghm	..	7 0	8 30	10 0	..	12 0	1 15	2 20	..	4 0	6 0	12 0	..	s. d.	s. d	, d.	s. d
9¼	Hampton	..	7 20	..	10 20	..	12 20	1 35	2 54	..	4 20	6 10	..	..	2 6	2 6	2 0	1 0
18¼	Coventry ..	..	7 47	9 12	10 47	..	12 47	2 4	3 29	..	4 47	6 47	12 47	..	5 0	4 6	4 0	3 0
23¼	Brandon ..	..	8 5	..	..	..	1 5	..	3 47	..	..	7 5	..	..	7 0	6 0	5 0	4 0
29¼	Rugby ..	..	8 23	9 43	11 17	..	1 23	2 35	4 13	4 0	5 17	7 23	1 23	1 0	8 6	8 0	6 6	5 0
37	Crick	..	8 50	..	..	..	1 50	..	4 41	..	..	7 50	..	..	11 0	10 0	8 6	6 6
42¾	Weedon ..	..	9 4	10 18	11 54	..	2 4	3 11	5 4	4 31	5 54	8 4	2 4	1 40	12 6	11 6	9 6	7 6
49¾	Blisworth .	..	9 27	..	12 16	..	2 28	3 35	5 28	4 55	6 16	8 27	2 28	2 0	14 6	13 0	11 0	8 6
52¼	Roade	.	9 35	..	..	..	2 38	..	5 37	..	..	8 35	..	..	15 6	14 0	11 6	9 6
59¾	Wolverton	6 45	9 55	11 5	12 40	..	3 0	4 0	6 15	5 20	6 40	8 55	2 55	2 30	17 6	16 0	13 6	10 6
65¾	Bletchley ..	6 58	10 21	..	..	..	3 26	..	6 37	..	..	9 20	..	..	19 6	17 6	15 0	12 0
71½	Leighton ..	7 14	10 37	..	1 16	..	3 42	..	6 58	..	7 16	9 37	..	..	21 0	19 0	16 0	12 6
	Aylesbury .	7 0	..	..	..	11 0	..	..	..	..	7 0	..	..	..		21 6		14 6
80½	Tring	7 41	11 4	12 6	1 42	11 26	4 11	5 0	7 30	6 21	7 42	10 4	4 1	3 35	23 6	21 6	18 0	14 6
84¼	B. Hampsd.	7 54	11 16	..	..	11 39	4 25	..	8 12	..	..	10 16	..	..	24 6	22 6	19 0	15 0
87¾	Boxmoor ...	8 4	11 25	..	..	11 49	4 34	..	8 27	..	..	10 25	..	..	25 6	23 6	19 6	15 6
94½	Watford ..	8 21	11 40	..	2 11	12 7	4 49	..	8 37	..	8 11	10 40	..	..	27 6	25 6	21 0	17 0
00¾	Harrow ..	8 39	11 55	...	..	12 24	5 7	..	9 7	..	..	10 55	..	..	29 6	27 0	22 6	18 0
12½	London ..	9 30	12 45	1 30	3 15	1 15	6 0	6 30	10 0	8 0	9 15	11 45	5 30	5 0	32 6	30 0	25 0	20 0

The 3rd class train takes passengers, private carriages, and horses, at the following charges—From Birmingham to London, Passengers 14s, carriages £3, horse boxes £4, and in proportion for intermediate stations.

Sunday Trains.—Mixed from Wolverton 6¾ a.m, Ml. 8½*§ a.m, Mixed 1½*‡‖ p.m. Mail, mix 12,*§ & 1 5‖‡ p.m. from Rugby.

* Trains in conjunction with the Grand Junction, Liverpool and Manchester. † Trains in cujunction with the Birmingham and Derby Junction, ‡ Trains in conjunction with the North Midland. § Trains in conjunction with the North Union and Lancaster and Preston Junction. ‖ Trains in conjunction with the Midland Counties, Leicester, Nottingham and Derby.

Passengers are especially recommended to have their names and address, or destination, *legibly written* on each part of their luggage, when it will be placed on the top of the coach in which they ride. If the passenger be destined to Liverpool or Manchester, and has booked his place through, his luggage will be placed on the Liverpool or Manchester coach, and will not be disturbed until it reaches its destination; and to prevent mistakes the passengers should show his ticket to the porters, and *see* that his luggage is placed on the proper coach.

A passenger having paid his fare, and taken out a ticket, may go by any of the trains of *that day*, but the ticket will not be available on the following day unless under special circumstances, when it may be exchanged for a new pass for the day required.

Fares and Times from Birmingham to London in 1841.

George Bradshaw

CHAPTER II

GEORGE BRADSHAW

No one will be surprised to hear that the Christian name of Mr. Bradshaw was George. Indeed, it is difficult to think what other name a man of his calibre could have had. So said Mr. Punch, and that is sufficient proof, if indeed proof were needed, that Bradshaw, like all great men, owed much to his parents. He was the only child of Thomas Bradshaw and his wife, Mary Rogers, who did all that their slender means would allow to give their son a good education. That is their title to fame. They may have been Bolton folk, for Mr. Charles Waring Bardsley says Bolton must be looked upon as the true home of four-fifths of our Bradshaws. If so, they gave the lie to the Lancashire historians who say that Mary Bradshaw, of the two husbands, was " the last of the Bradshaws," and failed to add:

> Other Bradshaws shall arise
> Heedless of a woman's name . . . .

George Bradshaw's first schoolmaster was a Swedenborgian Minister named Coward, but there is no reason for supposing that Bradshaw's Railway Time Tables were inspired by Swedenborg's writings on The Pleasures of Insanity.

Bradshaw was next sent to a school kept by a Mr. Scott, at Overton, Lancashire, and it was one of his greatest regrets in after life that his parents were unable to keep him there after the age of fourteen. It has been said he did not show much promise at school, and while he worked hard in later life to supply the gaps in his education, he did not, when success came, like some great fellows of the baser sort, say, "I was a dunce at school, but look at me now."

There is a little uncertainty about what happened after Bradshaw left school. Most writers follow the Dictionary of National Biography, which in turn is based on the notice in the Proceedings of the Institution of Civil Engineers written at the time of Bradshaw's death. According to these authorities, when his parents took Bradshaw away from school they apprenticed him to a Manchester engraver named Beale, who had made a reputation by his execution of the plates of Duncan Smith's four books of flourishings, entitled The Art of Penmanship Improved. When Mr. Beale, later in life, fell on evil days, Bradshaw, who had joined the Society of Friends at the age of 19, quietly did all he could to keep and comfort his old master in his poverty and distress. In 1820 the family removed to Belfast, where young George set up for himself as an engraver, but the venture did not prove a success, and after a year he returned to Manchester and began the engraving of maps.

Mr. C. T. Courtney Lewis, in The Story of Picture Printing in England during the Nineteenth Century, varies this account in some particulars:

> He was apprenticed to Thomas Tonbridge, an engraver of Market Street, Manchester, and when out of his time he went to Belfast to visit an uncle, thinking to establish himself in that city.

> He remained there two years, but, his plans not materialising, he returned to Manchester, and settled himself in offices in Market Place, where he remained until 1830, when he went to Cope's Court, off St. Mary's Gate. The site is now built over.

> The following year, i.e., 1831, William Blacklock, who was born in 1817, came as an apprentice.

> The business at first was mainly in engraving maps, but in 1835 a letterpress printing department was added.

> Blacklock's services became so valuable that he was made a partner even before he was twenty-one years of age.

> The firm of Bradshaw & Blacklock, as it then became, went to 27, Brown Street, Manchester, in 1839.

Many writers say that Bradshaw's first map was of his native county, Lancashire; but there is no mention of such a map in the Descriptive List of the Printed Maps of Lancashire, 1577-1900, compiled by Mr. Harold Whitaker, who searched all the Public Libraries of Lancashire and most of the likely ones in London.

He then compiled a map of the Canals of Lancashire and Yorkshire, which he dedicated to Telford in the following terms:—

G. Bradshaw's

Map of

Canals,

situated

in the Counties of

Lancaster, York, Derby & Chester;

shewing

The Heights of their Pools from a Level of 6ft. 10in.

under the old Dock Sill at Liverpool.

From Levels taken by

William Johnson and Son,

Manchester,

and

Dedicated by Permission

to

Thomas Telford, F.R.S.L. & E.,

President

of the Institution of Civil Engineers,

by his obliged

G. Bradshaw.

This Map, which showed the Railway or Tramway joining the North and South ends of the Lancaster Canal; the Liverpool and Manchester Railway; the St. Helens and Runcorn Gap Railway; the Warrington and Newton Railway; the Wigan Branch Railway; and the Bolton and Leigh

Railway, was sold, together with a Map of the Canals of the Midland Counties, entitled:—

G. Bradshaw's

Map of

Canals,

Navigable Rivers, Rail Roads, &c.,

in the Midland Counties of

England.

From Actual Survey

Shewing the Heights of the Ponds on the Lines of Navigation above the Low Water at

Liverpool.

From Levels taken by Twyford & Wilson, Surveyors & Engineers, Manchester.

Published by G. Bradshaw, Manchester, February 12th, 1829, and Sold by Mr. Jas. Gardner, 163, Regent Street, London.

Price Mounted on Rollers, £2 2s.   In Sheets, £1 11s. 6d.

Engraved & Printed

by W. R. Gardner,

13, Harpur Street,

London,

and with this Map of the Midland Counties was issued, in a limp green leather cover, a 20-page

Appendix

to

G. Bradshaw's Map

of the

Canals

and

Navigable Rivers

of the

Midland Counties

of

England.

———

Manchester:

Printed by A. Prentice, Market-Place.

———

1829.

This Appendix contained an Address:

At a period when the commercial relations are so much extended, and extending, it has often been considered a deficiency in our stores of national information that we had *no general map of Inland Navigation.* This deficiency we have undertaken to supply in some measure, and we flatter ourselves that the manner in which it has been executed, attended, as it necessarily must have been, by great expense and labour, will not be lost upon a discerning public.

We can assure our Subscribers that the work has been carefully examined by some of the ablest engineers in the kingdom, and compared with plans of their own; and they have declared their unqualified approbation of the accuracy of the accompanying Map.

Many important particulars, which could not with propriety be inserted in the body of the Map, will be found in the Appendix, which is designed to present, at " a bird's eye " glance, as it were, much information, without a reference to the Map itself, and, it is hoped, will be every way conducive to the ready consultation of the particulars for which the Map is designed.

It is trusted that the Legislator, as well as the Professional and Commercial Man, will find it in every respect to their satisfaction: and the Publisher takes this opportunity of thanking the numerous Subscribers for their liberal support to this first attempt to make the importance of our Inland Navigation obvious to all.

The Publisher is not aware that any inaccuracies exist in it; but if unfortunately any such should have occurred in a work of such extent, from any of those trifling causes which frequently baffle the most acute and attentive surveys, he will be happy to avail himself of any communication to that effect, and to correct the plates or renew them, as occasion may require.

Manchester,
February 28th, 1829.

A later edition of the Map of Lancashire and Yorkshire, dedicated to Telford, contained much more information and had a more elaborate border, and it was issued with a second edition of the Midland Counties, dated February 12th, 1830, and this Map, like its Northern companion, was also dedicated to Telford.

To complete the survey of the Canals of England, a Map, in three sections, of those in the Southern Counties was published in 1830, which shows the Surrey Railway and the Croydon & Merstham Railway. It is entitled:

G. Bradshaw's
Map of
Canals, Navigable Rivers,
Railways, &c.,
in the
Southern Counties
of
England.

From Actual Survey

shewing

The Heights of the Pools on the Lines of Navigation, also the Planes on the Railways from a Level of 6ft. 10in. under the old Dock Sill at Liverpool,

Dedicated by Permission to
Thomas Telford, F.R.S.L. & E.,
President of the Institution of Civil Engineers.

In the preparation of these Maps, which earned for him a great reputation, Bradshaw acquired a knowledge of surveying which brought him work from some members of the Institution of Civil Engineers, and it is a tribute to the greatness of Bradshaw that in February, 1842, he was made an Associate of that select body who had withheld membership from George Stephenson.

Sometime in 1828 there arrived in Manchester George Frederick Mandley, the " boy orator," a remarkable youth who corresponded with Robert Owen and Lord George Bentinck, wrote under the name "Quintus Hortensius," became High Chief Ranger of the Foresters, and Superintendent of Births,

Marriages and Deaths, and claimed that he had suggested to Bradshaw the publication of Railway Time Tables. A similar claim is made by some stained glass windows in the Higher Broughton Methodist Chapel, Great Cheetham Street West, Manchester, and in the Wesleyan Chapel, Aughton Road, Birkdale, near Southport, on behalf of Robert Diggles Kay, who was employed as a compositor by Bradshaw when he started a printer's business with W. T. Blacklock in 1837 or 1838. These windows are there to inform posterity that Kay was the originator and first Editor of Bradshaw, and those at Southport were unveiled by a gentleman who said: Mr. Kay, as most if not all of them knew, was the founder, originator and editor of a famous railway guide—Bradshaw's.

Now all the world knows that Bill Adams won the Battle of Waterloo, but while admiring Mr. Adams and all that he did, no one wishes to belittle the part the Duke of Wellington took in that affray, any more than Sir William Stirling Maxwell, who assisted at an eclipse, would have denied the Great Architect of the Universe His share in that celestial performance; and it is unfortunate that the perpetrators of those stained glass windows had not read the *Athenaeum* for January 17th, 1874, where Mr. Kay himself wrote: " Mr. Bradshaw suggested the idea " of the Time Table; or the *Manchester Guardian* for January 23rd, 1874, where he said, " Mr. Bradshaw suggested the idea to me in 1838." Kay was a good and faithful servant and was editor of the Guide from the start until 1880, for Bradshaw, like all successful men, picked a good man and let him get on with the job. Another man to whom Bradshaw owed much of his success was his London Agent, William James Adams, of 59, Fleet Street.

Adams, who was the son of a mathematical instrument maker, of No. 60, Fleet Street, was formerly in business as a general publisher at No. 170, Fleet Street, where he sold Guide Books and other travellers' necessaries ranging from passports to insect powder. No. 59, which was built about 1806, was first occupied by Daveson & Co., Perfumers, and in 1838 by Pigot & Co., publishers of directories, who, with prophetic insight of the uses to which their premises would be put, had included a Liverpool and Manchester Time Table for January, 1831, in their Manchester and Lancashire County Directory. Adams' business was taken over by Messrs. Blacklock, and No. 59 remained the London address of the Guide until December, 1905,

59, *Fleet Street, London*

when the firm removed to Surrey Street, Strand. The old house finally disappeared in 1907 during the rebuilding of Fleet Street.

But in addition to the rare gift of choosing men, Bradshaw had other valuable traits in his character. When his portrait by Richard Evans was bequeathed by his son Christopher to the National Portrait Gallery, a critic wrote:

> I cannot imagine Mr. Bradshaw ever missing a train. His face is that of a lover of order, accuracy and punctuality. The background of the portrait is appropriately a map of England with a network of Railway lines.

As a matter of fact, Bradshaw looks as though he never caught a train, but always travelled on the top of a coach, and the criticism suggests that the critic had the Guide rather than the portrait in mind. A better estimate of Bradshaw, the man, may be gained from the quiet but unmistakable determination of the following letters, in spite of the fact that they were written at a time when he was in failing health:

Railway Guide & General Printing & Stationery
Establishment,
Manchester, 47, Brown Street.

6th Mo., 22nd, 1850.

Dear Friend

(W. J. Adams),

I duly received thy kind letter just before I left home this morning. I feel grateful for the interest thou hast always shewn in my welfare.

I must confess I feel annoyed to hear that J. Darkin has not sufficient type to set up the sheet for the 2/6 edition; for many days previous to my leaving London I did all in my power to urge him, frequently telling him that I was certain that we had no time to spare and that he must be sure to see that he had type enough. It really does seem so unbusinesslike that I do not like it ; notwithstanding my indisposition I took care the moment I got here to have the various Plans and Maps put in hand and every exertion has been made to have them completed in time, and now to be told that we cannot get it out because the type was sent to Newton is really too bad. We *must* publish the 2/6 edition on the first and no mistake; if we have not type to set up the new matter it had better be sent to some other printer. J. Darkin will therefore please make his arrangements accordingly. I very much question if an office off the premises will answer; my principal reason for having J.D. at Fleet St. was that I might see any parties that might call about the Guide, now that cannot be accomplished I am inclined to view the matter differently. I conceive it will cost upwards of £4 a week to work the 2 Guides. This is a large sum and I question if McCorquodale & Co. will like to pay so much when they can have the thing done for so much less at Newton.

I am glad to say that I am improving in health nicely, but my hearing is much the same as when I left London. Hoping soon to be able to report more favourably in this respect.

I remain,

Sincerely thy friend,

G. BRADSHAW.

47, Brown Street,
Manchester,
6 Mo., 26/50.

Dear Friend
(Wm. Jas. Adams),

Surely there must be something wrong in James Darkin saying that he had sent me proofs of what he had done. I can only say that I have not seen any proofs and my partners say that they have not received any, if they have been sent to some other place than 47, Brown Street, immediate enquiries ought to be made—or send others without delay. It is pretty evident to me that I am to be thwarted in my endeavours to get out by the 1st. Please understand me, there is only *one* Map to be put into the shilling edition of the continental and that is the Central Europe; the Map of the Rhine is to go into the hand book or 2/6 edition. I have seen nothing of the one that Thauburn was to get up yet ; if it has been made up have the goodness to let me see it.

I am much pleased with the Specimen Glythography sent down and feel much inclined to have our guide map done in this way providing it was done in first rate style ; a second rate thing I would not have at any price. I now send one of our guide maps and shall be glad if thou wilt shew it to the party and ascertain what he would undertake to do it for; of course undertaking to do it equal or better if possible than the specimen sent.

I should like to know what number of impressions can be taken from the block without it being much worse or unfit to produce good maps.

The South Wales Railway is now open from Chepstow to Swansea, and we have not been furnished with a time bill. Please send to their office, 446, Strand, for one and let us have it per return.

I am still improving but do not hear much better yet. I am in hopes my hearing will get better as I gain strength.

I am, sincerely thy friend,

G. BRADSHAW.

To return to 1839—in that year Bradshaw published his first Railway Map, entitled:—

Map & Sections
of the
Railways
of
Great Britain.

Dedicated by Permission
to James Walker, F.R.S.L. & E.,
President of the Institution of Civil Engineers,
by George Bradshaw.

Published 1st Mo: 14, 1839, by G. Bradshaw,
Manchester, & Sold by J. Gardner,
Regent Street, London.

Engraved by I. Dower, Cumming Place, Pentonville, London.

The Map was accompanied by 28 pages of letterpress, the title page of which reads:—

Tables of The Gradients
to
Bradshaw's
Map of the Railways
of
Great Britain,
containing particulars of the
Lengths, Levels, and Gradients,
of all the Principal Railways in the Kingdom.

Dedicated to
James Walker, F.R.S.L. & E.,
President of the Institution of Civil Engineers.

Published 1st Mo: 14, 1839,
by George Bradshaw, Marys-Gate, Manchester,
and
Sold by James Gardner, Ordnance Map Seller, London.

This Map was corrected and enlarged from time to time and was described as:

a marvel of ingenuity and the fruit of a really admirable enterprise. It constitutes a visible epitome of the mighty conquests made by the Anglo-Saxon race in their memorable march—a march not of decades, but of centuries—along the broad and holy track of civilisation.

Bradshaw sent a copy of this marvel to the London & Birmingham Railway with the following letter:—

1, Savoy Steps, Strand,
June 3rd, 1839.

Sir,

Messrs. Bradshaw & Co. have done themselves the pleasure of waiting upon you in order to submit to your Notice their new & splendid Map of all the Railways wh. the sections, gradients, &c., thereof, with all the Canals & public roads, the lines finish'd constructing & in contemplation—of Great Britain—for which the Company did them the Honour of subscribing when in contemplation. They humbly trust that it will give you that satisfaction they have endeavoured to deserve.

We have to be Sir,
Your obed't serv'ts,

Price £3 3 0.   G. BRADSHAW & CO.
Wh. Books of Tables.

This letter, which might serve as a new model for those boring people who " solicit a continuance of our esteemed commands," is also interesting from the fact that it is dated " June " and not " 6th Mo." For Bradshaw, being a Quaker, believed all he could of religion, but unlike Rousseau, did not respect the rest. Consequently, he referred to the months by numbers, like soldiers, with their pagan names confined to brackets—a practice wisely followed by the present Proprietors, for Custom, like Bradshaw, is the great guide of human life. But if I were April's lady, or flaming June, I should take it a little unfair that the week-day Deities do not come within the ambit of this strange interdict; for those bad men, Woden and Thor, are merely abbreviated to Weds. and Thurs. only, and escape damnatory notation.

In addition to Calendar Reform, Bradshaw showed the faith that was in him by works of a more practical character. He realised that perpetual devotion to what a man calls his business is only to be sustained by perpetual neglect of many other things, and during the last six years of his life was content to leave the work connected with the Guide to his able editor Kay and his zealous agent Adams.

In spite of failing health he devoted himself actively to philanthropy:

Anything that had for its object the good of mankind, found in him a ready advocacy and help, and this in no narrow or sectarian spirit; for although his charity was so unostentatious as scarcely to be known beyond the circles in which it was exercised, his benevolence was so universal as to know no limit but his means and opportunity.

On the 6th September, 1853, while staying at Christiania, whither he had gone to visit an old Manchester acquaintance, Mr. Stephen B. Shaw, Manager of the Norwegian Railway, and a Mr. Bennet, the Norwegian prototype of Thomas Cook & Son, he was seized with Asiatic cholera and died within a few hours.

His friend Elihu Burritt, the learned blacksmith, who taught himself to read nearly fifty languages, fortunately wrote his obituary in English:

How few, comparatively, will ever know and appreciate his worth ! How few, even in the Town in which he lived, will ever know the value of his busy life of quiet benevolence ! His meek walks of charity are marked by no monument bearing his name; they may have left few footprints visible to human eye; but they dropped the dew of Christian love among the dwellings of poverty and ignorance: and he did not even let his left hand know what his right hand did for these. He was ever planning secretly little enterprises of good-will to them, which should ameliorate their condition and bring to them light and comfort. But it was in connexion with the various operations embraced in the peace movement that we were brought into intimate acquaintance and connexion with him. In this great field of philanthropy he never wearied, but waxed warmer and brighter in faith and activity to the last. Here too, he laboured with the characteristic modesty of his gentle spirit and he was always ready to take upon himself the most burdensome, or mechanical part of the work. Well do we remember the interesting incidents of a short railway ride from Manchester to Bolton on the 23rd February, 1848, the day before the news of the last French Revolution reached England. On our way we suggested the idea of holding a Peace Conference in Paris during the approaching summer. As we discussed the proposition the element of expense seemed to affect its practicability. The cost of the journey to Paris and back would in a great measure determine the number of delegates to such a Conference. Mr. Bradshaw immediately took out his pencil, and, on the crown of his hat, commenced an estimate of the expenses of the excursion, and the charges in Paris to each delegate. His acquaintance and connexion with the Railway Companies in England and France enabled him to make an accurate computation of the cost; and before our short ride was terminated he had set it down at £5 per head, the actual charge which was paid by the delegates to the Conference in Paris in 1849. Circumstances, which we need not describe, constrained the friends of peace to hold their first grand meeting on the Continent in Brussels, in 1848. Mr. Bradshaw immediately volunteered to assist in making the necessary preparations and proceeded forthwith to the City in company with John Scoble, Esq. He took chiefly upon himself the onerous and rather difficult task of providing for the cheap and expeditious conveyance of delegates from England by special steam packet and railway train, and for their accommodation at the hotels. No one, we are confident, who was present on that·interesting occasion, will forget his indefatigable activity and devotion in this important department of the enterprise. He took upon himself a still larger task the next year, in connexion with the great Peace Congress in Paris. Nearly seven hundred persons were conveyed by special trains and steamers from London to attend that memorable meeting. The arrangements for their transportation, refreshments by the way, and accommodation in Paris, imposed a very onerous task upon our dear friend; and the imperturbable patience and good-will with which he discharged it, illustrated one of the beautiful traits of his character. He performed a similar service in connexion with the Peace Congress at Frankfort the following year; and assisted, in the same spirit of self-sacrifice, in the preparations for the great meeting in London in 1851. The demonstration for 1852 was postponed to January, 1853, and was held in his own town of Manchester. His labour and zeal to promote its success were indefatigable; and his good and great heart seemed to rejoice exceedingly at the result. When the proposition was brought forward to raise a fund of £10,000 in order to extend the operations of the Peace movement, he generously subscribed £500. No sooner had this Peace Conference been brought to a close than he began to lend a helping hand to the Ocean Penny Postage Bazaar in Manchester. From the outset he entered heart and soul into this postal reform, and was ready to advance it to the utmost extent of his ability. He was also deeply interested in the Olive Leaf Mission, and was delighted to hear the report of its progress, which was presented at the soirée in the Bridge House Hotel, London, on the 24th of May. That was the last time we saw his face. Towards the close of the summer we both went on the Continent, partly to recruit for future labours in the cause. Our routes were different, but we had intended to visit the very countries to which he journied. But hearing of the fearful prevalence of the cholera in Denmark, Sweden, and Norway, we concluded to proceed no farther north than Hamburgh. While we were in that city, and little dreaming of such a dispensation, George Bradshaw was seized by the fatal malady in Christiania, in Norway, and, in a few hours, his useful life was extinguished on earth. Far from home and kin he yielded up his spirit into the hands of his Redeemer, whom he had followed and served with such single-hearted devotion. That honest and generous heart, that beat with such earnest sympathies for every enterprise and effort of philanthropy, has been stilled for ever on earth. His lowly grave lies in a foreign land, seldom visited by his countrymen. Few, if any, of his friends will ever see where they laid him down to rest. We trust some humble stone may mark the spot and that now and anon some one who knew his worth may commune with the mysteries of immortality over that precious dust.

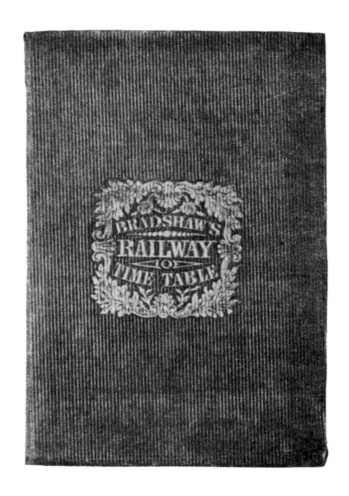

Cover of first Time Table,
1839

BRADSHAW'S

Railway Companion,

CONTAINING

THE TIMES OF DEPARTURE,

FARES, &c.

OF THE RAILWAYS IN ENGLAND,

AND ALSO

Hackney Coach Fares

FROM THE PRINCIPAL RAILWAY STATIONS,

ILLUSTRATED WITH

MAPS OF THE COUNTRY THROUGH WHICH THE
RAILWAYS PASS,

AND PLANS OF

LONDON, BIRMINGHAM, LEEDS.

LIVERPOOL, AND MANCHESTER.

PRICE ONE SHILLING.

MANCHESTER :

PRINTED & PUBLISHED BY BRADSHAW & BLACKLOCK.
27, BROWN-STREET; AND SOLD BY

. R. GROOMBRIDGE, PATERNOSTER ROW, LONDON ;
AND ALL BOOKSELLERS AND RAILWAY COMPANIES

1841.

CHAPTER III

THE STRANGE COMPANIONS

" To live is to change, and to be perfect is to have changed often," but those who feel they cannot go all the way to Rome with Cardinal Newman can at any rate prove the truth of his statement by a study of the evolution of Bradshaw's Railway Time Tables.

Herbert Spencer in his autobiography, published in 1904, says, " Bradshaw's Guide did not commence till the autumn of 1838, when it made its appearance in the shape of some three or four leaves. There have been disputes as to the date of its origin, but I speak from definite remembrance." He had written at greater length in *The Athenaeum* on January 26th, 1889, when he said, " I was a civil engineer, engaged on the London and Birmingham . . . . Before the end of September, 1838, I left for the purpose of joining the staff of the Birmingham and Gloucester at Worcester. I have a distinct recollection that before I left I saw Bradshaw's Time Tables at the Euston Station. How much earlier this may have been I do not know, but it was certainly before the end of September."

Spencer is borne out by Christopher Bradshaw, one of Bradshaw's sons, who wrote in the *Figaro* of January 21st, 1874: " It was commenced as Bradshaw's Railway Companion in the autumn of 1838," and writing in the *Southport Visiter* on September 15th, 1898, he explained that the idea came to Bradshaw soon after the opening of the Liverpool and Manchester Railway, that he often discussed it with his friends, and that it began to take practical shape in 1837 when, in conjunction with W. T. Blacklock, he added letterpress printing to his business of map engraving. But the most circumstantial account is given by Henry Diggles Kay, the first editor of the Guide. In *Tit-Bits* of February 24th, 1883, Kay wrote:

> In the early part of 1838 I received an appointment from Mr. George Bradshaw, engraver, copperplate and lithographic printer, Cope's Court, St. Mary's Gate, Manchester, to inaugurate the letterpress printing, which he was anxious to have added to his other engagements. He had already acquired considerable notoriety by his large canal maps of Great Britain, in the publication of which he had been very successful. About six weeks after the initiation of the letterpress department,

Mr. W. T. Blacklock became a partner, and the name of the firm changed to that of Bradshaw & Blacklock . . . . It was in the middle of 1838 when Mr. Bradshaw handed me one of the Liverpool and Manchester passenger time bills to condense into a form and size suitable for the waistcoat pocket. The information thus prepared was put into a stiff cover, accompanied by a map of Great Britain and labelled Bradshaw's Railway Time Table. The idea was suggested in order to create a sale for a large number of maps of England and Wales which he had in stock, lying idle. The first edition was quickly sold, the second and third equally so. In the meantime, I was making additions in the shape of railway information, etc., so that by the 19th October, 1839, we had a really most compact and useful little railway guide, containing, with the title and address, eight pages of railway matter and cab fares, and five pages of maps and plans. Before the end of 1840, it contained twenty pages of railway and other matter, and twelve pages of maps and plans, price 1s., and the title changed to Bradshaw's Railway Companion.

Christopher Bradshaw's evidence is admittedly second-hand and there are those who assert that what Spencer and Kay *remembered* is not evidence at all. Like the man from Sheffield, they say, " Show it me," joyful in the knowledge that no specimen of these early time tables is known to have survived. The earliest surviving copy of Bradshaw's Railway Time Tables is dated 10th Mo. 19th, 1839, and therefore the 19th October, 1939, is the earliest centenary that can be celebrated with certainty, but to doubt Spencer's and Kay's words because they are merely reminiscences is like denying the existence of Lady Macbeth's poor cat because time has mislaid the adage.

Mention has been made in the first chapter of the early guide books of individual lines, and that there was no call for a general Railway Time Table until the complete opening of the London and Birmingham Railway in September, 1838. A month or so previously James Drake, of Birmingham, published a folder containing Regulations, Time, Fare, and Distance Tables of the London and Birmingham, Grand Junction and Liverpool and Manchester Companies. Price 4d. in a neat case for the pocket. In February, 1839, " Bridgen's Time Table of the Grand Junction and London and Birmingham Railways" appeared, "a very neat and exceedingly useful sixpenny work, published at Wolverhampton in a form which renders it suitable for the waistcoat pocket." Eight months after, on October 5th, 1839, a new edition was advertised: "This day is published, price 6d., done up in cloth, in so concise a way as to be adapted for the waistcoat pocket, Bridgen's Time Table of the London & Birmingham, Grand Junction, Birmingham & Derby, Bolton, Liverpool & Manchester, the North Union, and the Manchester and Leeds Railways."

A later edition, dated March 30th, 1840, was done up in so concise a way as to measure 2 inches by 4, and was produced in the same strange manner as Bradshaw's Companion of that year. It gave the times of the trains of the

> Grand Junction,
> London and Birmingham,
> Birmingham and Derby,
> Liverpool and Manchester,
> Manchester, Bolton, and Bury,
> North Union,
> Manchester and Leeds,
> Great Western,
> Southern,
> Eastern Counties,
> London and Greenwich, and
> London and Croydon Railways.

Mr. James Drake's and Mr. Joseph Bridgen's little systems had their day and ceased to be, and so did that of Mr. John Gadsby, but his case is rather different. Gadsby started business in 1834 as a printer in Manchester, and became printer and publisher to the Anti-Corn Law League. The minutes of the Liverpool and Manchester Railway of August 12th, 1839, record:

> "Read a letter from Mr. John Gadsby, of Newalls Buildings, Manchester, asking permission to print and sell Lists of the Times of Departures of the Liverpool and Manchester and Grand Junction trains—The publication to take place with the sanction of the Directors of the different Companies. The Board was

of opinion that such a List of Departures published under proper regulations, would prove a great convenience to the public, and the Treasurer was authorised to afford proper facilities to the publisher to obtain correct Lists, as often as need be, of the times of Departures of the Liverpool and Manchester trains.''

The Time Tables duly appeared in January, 1840, and Gadsby lived unhappily ever after because nobody would believe him when he said that he had been first in the field.

The notion of printing general railway time tables had possibly occurred to the various publishers from the fact that Railways used to advertise the times of the trains in the newspapers, which was not a convenient or portable form for travellers. The desire to publish time tables even spread to the Post Office London Directory, which in its anxiety to serve the public overlooked the fact that times might be changed during the year. In those days Mr. Frederic Kelly dated his letters from the General Post Office.

Bradshaw did not write to the Liverpool and Manchester Railway as Gadsby did. According to Kay, he obtained a copy of their time tables in 1838 and told Kay to arrange them in a portable form. They must have been in a perishable form also, for no copy is known to have survived, possibly because they had no protecting cover. What has survived is the little book dated 10th Mo. 19th, 1839. It is in a green cloth cover 3 inches by $4\frac{1}{2}$, with the words, Bradshaw's Railway Time Table, in a design of golden foliage. The word Time Table has become plural in the title page, which is followed by an address, and the contents are:

> Map of the Railways in Lancashire, &c.,
> Liverpool to Manchester Time Table,
> Plan of Liverpool,
> Manchester to Liverpool Time Table,
> Plan of Manchester,
> Manchester to Littleborough Time Table,
> Map of Railways in Yorkshire,
> York to Leeds and Selby Time Table,
> Plan of Leeds,
> North Union Time Table,
> Manchester to Bolton Time Table, and
> Liverpool Hackney Coach Fares.

BRADSHAW'S

Railway Time Tables,

AND ASSISTANT TO

RAILWAY TRAVELLING,

WITH

ILLUSTRATIVE MAPS & PLANS.

AUTHOR OF

BRADSHAW'S MAP AND SECTION OF THE
RAILWAYS OF GREAT BRITAIN,
5FT. 4IN. BY 3FT. 4IN.

Price in Sheets . . . 1 11 6
Mounted 2 10 0

AND SOLD BY G. BRADSHAW, BROWN-STREET,
MANCHESTER;
AND WYLD, CHARING CROSS, LONDON.

PRICE SIXPENCE.

LONDON:

SHEPHERD AND SUTTON, AND WYLD,
CHARING CROSS,

AND SOLD BY ALL BOOKSELLERS AND
RAILWAY COMPANIES.

10th Mo. 19th, 1839.

ADDRESS.

THIS Book is published by the assistance of the several Railway Companies, on which account the information it contains may be depended upon as being correct and authentic. The necessity of such a work is so obvious as to need no apology; and the merits of it can be best ascertained by a reference to the execution both as regards the style and correctness of the Maps and Plans with which it is illustrated.

The next edition of this work will be published on the 1st of 1st Mo. 1840; and succeeding Editions will appear every three months, with such alterations as have been made in the interval.

The manner in which the pages were assembled was unusual, but not unique, for Mr. Bridgen, of Wolverhampton, adopted the same plan.

The Title Page, Address, Time Tables and Maps were printed on one side of the paper only, each piece of paper being the size of two pages of the book. They were then folded like a piece of notepaper with the printing inside, and then they were pasted together back to back, the first and last sheets being pasted on to the inside of the covers. By this means stitching was unnecessary, and it was possible to bring the book up to date by buying a sheet of the time tables each month, cutting them out and pasting them over the obsolete pages. This practice was adopted and advertised at a later date, but the fact that the Time Tables in book form were produced in this unusual way from the start, suggests that Spencer and Kay were right ; and that the books were a later development of the earlier sheets.

BRADSHAW'S

𝕽𝖆𝖎𝖑𝖜𝖆𝖞 𝕿𝖎𝖒𝖊 𝕿𝖆𝖇𝖑𝖊𝖘,

AND ASSISTANT TO

RAILWAY TRAVELLING,

WITH

ILLUSTRATIVE MAPS & PLANS.

AUTHOR OF

BRADSHAW'S MAP AND SECTION OF THE
RAILWAYS OF GREAT BRITAIN,
5FT. 4IN. BY 3FT. 4IN.

| PRICE IN SHEETS | . . . | 1 11 6 |
| MOUNTED | . . . . . | 2 10 0 |

AND SOLD BY G. BRADSHAW, BROWN-STREET,
MANCHESTER;
AND WYLD, CHARING CROSS, LONDON.

PRICE SIXPENCE.

LONDON :

SHEPHERD AND SUTTON, AND WYLD,
CHARING CROSS,

AND SOLD BY ALL BOOKSELLERS AND
RAILWAY COMPANIES.

10th Mo. 25th, 1839. (No. 2)

ADDRESS.

THIS Book is published by the assistance of the several Railway Companies, on which account the information it contains may be depended upon as being correct and authentic. The necessity of such a work is so obvious as to need no apology; and the merits of it can be best ascertained by a reference to the execution both as regards the style and correctness of the Maps and Plans with which it is illustrated.

The next edition of this work will be published on the 1st of 1st Mo. 1840; and succeeding Editions will appear every three months, with such alterations as have been made in the interval.

There were three issues of the first book, all dated 10th Mo., 19th, 1839, the later ones containing minor alterations, and the last issue was reprinted in 1889, on the occasion of its Jubilee. The original edition had yellow end-papers, in the reprint the title page is pasted on the inside of the cover and there are no end-papers. There is nothing to indicate that it is a facsimile reprint, though it is a quarter-of-an-inch larger each way than the original, but

'Tis sweet to know there is an eye will mark

. Our coming, and look brighter when we come,

and when an original Bradshaw of 10th Mo., 19th, 1839, is produced it is clear that "None but himself can be his parallel." He is his own guarantee.

Another facsimile was published twelve years later, bearing the imprint: "Reprinted by Henry Blacklock & Company, Printers & Publishers of Bradshaw's Guides, 1901," but in this case the cover did not bear the impressed design of the golden leaves but a little gilt label of later issue was

38

pasted on to it. Both reprints are frequently mistaken for originals, especially when an original fetches a big price in the Sale Rooms. On February 25th, 1901, an original fetched £25 at Sotheby's. The announcement made people turn out their cupboards, and nowadays £1 is a more usual price.

It will have been noticed that the Time Tables in the first book of 10th Mo., 19th, 1839, were for the trains on the Liverpool and Manchester and Northern Lines.

On 10th Mo., 25th, 1839, Bradshaw published another book for the Southern Lines, including:

Map of Warwickshire and Northamptonshire,
Map of Bedford and Hertford,
London to Birmingham Time Table,
Birmingham to London Time Table,
Plan of Birmingham,
Birmingham to Liverpool and Manchester Time Table,
Liverpool to Manchester and Birmingham Time Table,
Map of Salop and Stafford,
Liverpool to Manchester Time Table,
Manchester to Liverpool Time Table,
Plan of Manchester,
Map of the Railways in Lancashire,
Abridged Time Tables—
    Birmingham and Derby,
    Manchester and Leeds,
    Manchester, Bolton and Bury,
    North Union Railway,
    Nottingham and Derby,
    Sheffield and Rotherham,
Thompson's Table showing the rate of travelling per hour,
Great Western Railway Time Table,
Hackney Coach Fares from Euston Station, London, and
Cab Fares from the Railway Station, Birmingham.

Thompson's Table is an interesting mystery. Nobody knows who Thompson was. By the 1st January, 1840, he was unimportant enough to have his name dropped from his tables, and in several issues of the Companion of that year the words Rochdale Station appear at the bottom of the table.

THOMPSON'S TABLE,

SHEWING THE RATE OF TRAVELLING PER HOUR.

A Quarter of a Mile in		Equals Miles per Hour.	A Quarter of a Mile in		Equals Miles per Hour.	A Quarter of a Mile in		Equals Miles per Hour.
Min.	Sec.		Min.	Sec.		Min.	Sec.	
15	..	1	..	44	20½	..	24¼	37
7	30	2	..	43	21	..	23½	38
5	..	3	..	42	21½	..	23	39
3	45	4	..	41	22	..	22½	40
3	..	5	..	40	22½	..	22	41
2	30	6	..	39	23	..	21½	42
2	8	7	..	38	23½	..	21	43
1	52	8	..	37	24	..	20½	44
1	40	9	..	36½	24½	..	20	45
1	30	10	..	36	25	..	18	50
1	22	11	..	35	25½	..	17	52
1	15	12	..	34	26	..	16	56
1	9	13	..	33½	26½	..	15	60
1	4	14	..	33	27	..	14	64
1	..	15	..	32½	27½	..	13	69
..	58	15½	..	32	28	..	12	75
..	56	16	..	31½	28½	..	11¼	80
..	54½	16½	..	31	29	..	10	90
..	53	17	..	30½	29½	..	9	100
..	51½	17½	..	30	30	..	7½	120
..	50	18	..	29	31	..	6	150
..	48½	18½	..	28	32	..	4½	200
..	47	19	..	27¼	33	..	2¼	400
..	46	19½	..	26½	34			
..	45	20	..	25	36			

Great Western Railway.

London to Twyford—8, 9, 10, 12, a.m.; 2, 4, 5, 6, 7, 8, p.m.
Sunday Trains—8, 9, a.m.; 5, 7, p.m.
Twyford to London—6, 9, 10, 12, a.m.; 2, 4, 5, 6, 7, 8, p.m.
Sunday Trains—6, 9, a.m.; 5, 7, p.m.
Fares—1st class, 7s.; 2nd class, 5s.

TABLE

SHEWING THE RATE OF TRAVELLING PER HOUI

A Quarter of a Mile in		Equals Miles per Hour	A Quarter of a Mile in		Equals Miles per Hour.	A Quarter of a Mile in		Equa Mile per Hour
Min.	Sec.		Min.	Sec.		Min.	Sec.	
15		1	.	44	20½	..	24¼	37
7	30	2	..	43	21	.	23½	38
5		3	.	42	21½		23	39
3	45	4		41	22		22½	40
3	.	5		40	22½		22	41
2	30	6	.	39	23		21½	42
2	8	7	..	38	23½	.	21	43
6	52	8	.	37	24	.	20½	44
1	40	9		36½	24½		20	45
1	30	10		36	25	.	18	50
1	22	11	..	35	25½	..	17	52
1	15	12	.	34	26	..	16	56
1	9	13	.	33½	26½	..	15	60
1	4	14	..	33	27	..	14	64
1	..	15	..	32½	27½	..	13	69
..	58	15½	..	32	28	..	12	75
..	56	16	..	31½	28½	..	11¼	80
..	54½	16½	..	31	29	..	10	90
..	53	17	..	30½	29½	..	9	100
..	51½	17½	..	30	30	..	7½	120
..	50	18	..	29	31	..	6	150
.	48½	18½	..	28	32	..	4½	200
..	47	19	..	27¼	33	..	2¼	400
..	46	19½	..	26½	34			
..	45	20	..	25	36			

On *all* Railways the distances are distinctly pointed out by posts erected each quarter of a mile; the rate of speed can be ascertained at once by refering to the above table.

Rochdale Station.

Now one of the difficulties in opening a new Railway in the early days was to find experienced men to work it, consequently there was a tendency to entice men away from the older companies. In April, 1839, there was trouble between the Manchester and Leeds and the Newcastle and Carlisle Companies over a Mr. George Thompson, who had left the service of the latter Company to be in at the opening of the Manchester and Leeds, and it is possible he was the first Station Master at Rochdale and the compiler of the Rate of Travelling Tables. On the other hand, in the construction of the Manchester and Leeds Railway, the Rochdale Contract was let to Messrs. Thompson & Turner, and it may have been Mr. Thompson, the Contractor, who compiled the Table.

BRADSHAW'S

Railway Time Tables,

AND ASSISTANT TO

RAILWAY TRAVELLING,

WITH

ILLUSTRATIVE MAPS & PLANS.

AUTHOR OF

BRADSHAW'S MAP AND SECTION OF THE
RAILWAYS OF GREAT BRITAIN,
5FT. 4IN. BY 3FT. 4IN.

PRICE IN SHEETS . . .	1	11	6
MOUNTED	2	10	0

AND SOLD BY G. BRADSHAW, BROWN-STREET,
MANCHESTER;
AND WYLD, CHARING CROSS, LONDON.

PRICE ONE SHILLING.

LONDON :

SHEPHERD AND SUTTON, AND WYLD,
CHARING CROSS,
AND SOLD BY ALL BOOKSELLERS AND
RAILWAY COMPANIES.

10th Mo. 25th, 1839.   **(No. 3)**

ADDRESS.

THIS Book is published by the assistance of the several Railway Companies, on which account the information it contains may be depended upon as being correct and authentic. The necessity of such a work is so obvious as to need no apology; and the merits of it can be best ascertained by a reference to the execution both as regards the style and correctness of the Maps and Plans with which it is illustrated.

The next edition of this work will be published on the 1st of 1st Mo. 1840; and succeeding Editions will appear every three months, with such alterations as have been

The Southern Time Table of 10th Mo., 25th, 1839, had the figure (2) at the bottom of the title page, and on the same date Bradshaw published yet another time table with the figure (3) at the bottom of the title page. This third time table was a combination of the two previous companion volumes, and possibly for that reason was called Bradshaw's Railway Companion on the outside cover. Possibly not! There is still a better reason for the change of name. It may have been called *Companion* to distinguish it from the two previous volumes, but as henceforth the time tables in book form were only published in the combined form and under the name *Companion*, the change may have been to distinguish the Book from the Time Tables in sheet form, of which Spencer and Kay speak, and which certainly were published later.

There were several variations of Nos. 2 and 3. Indeed, from the odd way in which the sheets were pasted together Bradshaw's method might be described as "bespoke" publishing. Every selling agent seems to have had his private imprint, and copies are found with the following names on the title pages:

> Shepherd & Sutton and Wyld, Charing Cross,
> Shepherd & Sutton, Priest Court, Foster Lane, Cheapside,
> Chas. Tilt, Fleet Street,
> C. Davies & Co., North John Street, Liverpool,
> John M. Knott, 5, Bude Court, London,
> Henry Lacy, Bold Street, Liverpool,
> Henry Mosley & Sons, Derby,
> Darton & Clarke, Holborn,
> Tilt & Bogue, Fleet Street,
> S. E. Mayhew, 5, Somers Town Terrace, Ossulston Street, near the Euston Station,

and Mr. Harris, of Hatton Garden, had his name on the labels on the outside of the covers of those sold by him.

Like No. 1, No. 3 was reproduced, and these reproductions are reputed to have been made by what is known as the photolitho process, a very remarkable form of photography, because in reproducing No. 3 the word "Bedford," indicating the County, and running up the map in the original, is reversed and runs down the map in the reproduction. Here again "bespoke" publishing may be the explanation, as in the Companion of the 1st January, 1840, the original maps are still being used, while in those of 1841 and subsequently the new form is found.

The Time Tables of 10th Mo., 19th, 1839, and No. 2 of 10th Mo., 25th, 1839, were price 6d. each, while the combination of the first two, No. 3 of 10th Mo., 25th, 1839, cost 1/-.

Henceforth they were named *Companion* on the title page as well as the cover, and still continue to supply surprises for the bibliophile and insoluble problems for the bibliographer.

One of the editions of No. 3 was dated December 14th, 1839, and three days later the following letter was sent to the Secretary of the London and Birmingham Railway:

Manchester, 12 Mo., 17th, 1839,
47, Brown Street.

Respected Friend,

Herewith thou hast a copy of our Railway Companion which we have pleasure to state has had an unprecedented sale and beg thine acceptance of it; as it is our intention to publish a second Edition *immediately*, we shall esteem it a favour if thou wilt examine the Table in reference to the time of starting, etc., and if any change or alteration should be likely to occur within the next three months we shall feel highly favoured by receiving that information; or if any thing could be done that (in thy opinion) would make the work more useful or interesting, if thou wilt take the trouble to suggest it, we should be most happy to adopt the plan.

This work will be *uniformly* published every Three months, and the next Edition must be out on or before the first day of the year 1840, it will therefore be essentially necessary for us to have all the help we can get by the 24th Instant. Should any of the Gentlemen in the Establishment feel disposed to have a few dozen for sale at any of the Stations (a custom now become very general), we should have much pleasure in supplying them at 25 per ct. off the selling price.

I am, respectfully, Sir,
per pro BRADSHAW & BLACKLOCK,
Your obedt. St.,
Rd. Renshaw.

The unprecedented sale explains why so many issues of the first three volumes were made, and the use of the word "unprecedented" suggests that the time tables had previously been issued in the form remembered by Spencer and Kay. The second edition to which Renshaw refers must have

BRADSHAW'S

Railway Companion,

CONTAINING

THE TIMES OF DEPARTURE,

FARES, &c.

OF THE RAILWAYS IN ENGLAND,

AND ALSO

Hackney Coach Fares

FROM THE PRINCIPAL RAILWAY STATIONS,

ILLUSTRATED WITH

MAPS OF THE COUNTRY THROUGH WHICH THE
RAILWAYS PASS,

AND PLANS OF

LONDON, BIRMINGHAM, LEEDS,

LIVERPOOL, AND MANCHESTER.

PRICE ONE SHILLING.

MANCHESTER :

PRINTED & PUBLISHED BY BRADSHAW & BLACKLOCK
27, BROWN-STREET ; AND SOLD BY
C. DAVIES, NORTH JOHN-STREET LIVERPOOL,
AND ALL BOOKSELLERS AND RAILWAY COMPANIES.

1840.

ADDRESS.

THIS Book is published with the assistance
of the several Railway Companies, on which
account the information it contains may be
depended upon as being correct and authentic.
The necessity for such a work is so obvious
as to need no apology, and the merits of it
can be best ascertained by a reference to the
execution both as regards the style and correctness of the Maps and Plans with which
it is illustrated.

To Railway Companies.

G. BRADSHAW would feel particularly
obliged by an intimation being forwarded to
him at 27, Brown-street, Manchester, of any
change in Fares or Times of Departure, on
any of the Lines, in order that the correction
may be immediately made in the work.

been the Companion of the 1st January, 1840, with the name Companion on
the title page as well as on the cover, and with an altered address.

Renshaw appears to have been the editor and Kay at this time was
possibly still a compositor.

The intention to publish every three months was frustrated from the
start by the fact that new lines were being opened almost daily. The
following list of openings is taken from Bradshaw's Shareholders' Manual of
1849, and well illustrates the nature of the problem which Bradshaw so
efficiently handled:

1832.	Apl.	10.	Dundee & Newtyle opened.
1836.	Dec.	14.	London & Greenwich opened.
1837.	Jul.	6.	Grand Junction opened.
1838.	May	31.	Manchester & Bolton opened.
	Jun.	5.	Great Western partly opened.
	,,	18.	Newcastle & Carlisle opened.
	Sep.	17.	London & Birmingham Railway opened throughout.
	Oct.	20.	Durham Junction opened.
	,,	22.	North Union & Preston opened.
	,,	30.	Sheffield & Rotherham opened.
1839.	Jan.	3.	Arbroath & Forfar opened.
	Jun.	14.	London & Croydon opened.
	Aug.	11.	Birmingham & Derby opened.
1840.	Jan.	8.	Chester & Birkenhead completed.
	Apl.	1.	Dundee, Perth & Aberdeen Junction (16¾ m.) opened.
	May	3.	Preston & Longridge opened.
	,,	11.	South Western opened throughout.
	Jun.	20.	Newcastle & North Shields.
	,,	29.	Midland Counties opened.
	,,	30.	York & North Midland opened.
	Jul.	13.	Glasgow & Ayr opened.
	,,	14.	Maryport & Carlisle opened.
	,,	17.	Preston & Wyre opened.
	Sep.	15.	Northern & Eastern partly opened.
	Oct.	9.	Taff Vale partly opened.
	Nov.	13.	Stockton & Hartlepool opened.
1841.	Jan.	2.	London & Blackwell completed.
	,,	4.	Birmingham & Gloucester completed.
	Jun.	26.	Lancaster & Preston Junction opened.
	Sep.	22.	Chester & Birkenhead opened.
	Oct.	1.	Chester & Crewe opened.
1842.	Feb.	5.	Durham & Sunderland opened.
	,,	6.	Edinburgh & Glasgow opened.
1843.	Feb.	7.	Glasgow, Kilmarnock & Ayr opened.
	Mar.	29.	Eastern Counties opened.
	Jun.	22.	Bolton & Preston opened.
1844.	Jan.	5.	Bristol & Gloucester opened.
	,,	9.	Dublin & Drogheda completed.
	Feb.	9.	Yarmouth & Norwich opened.

1844	May	1.	Bricklayers Arms Extn. (S.E.) opened.
(continued)	,,	2.	G.W. opened to Exeter.
	,,	4.	Liverpool & Leeds Junction opened.
	Dec.	3.	Warwick & Leamington opened.
1845.	Jul.	27.	Eastern Counties opened to Cambridge and Ely.
	Sep.	13.	Her Majesty's Railway at Gosport opened.
1846.	Apl.	14.	Lancashire & Yorkshire (Ashton Branch) opened.
	May	26.	Exeter to Teignmouth opened.
	Jun.	1.	East Lancashire, Blackburn to Preston, opened.
	,,	15.	Eastern Union opened.
	Aug.	6.	Nottingham & Lincoln opened.
	Sep.	3.	Syston & Melton Mowbray opened.
	,,	28.	East Lancashire, Manchester to Rawtenstall, opened.
	Oct.	3.	Stamford & Peterborough opened.
	,,	4.	Hull & Bridlington opened.
	,,	27.	Lynn & Downham Branch opened.
	Nov.	3.	Shrewsbury & Chester opened to Ruabon.
	Dec.	1.	S. East Margate Branch ($3\frac{1}{2}$ m.) opened.
	,,	17.	Lancaster & Carlisle opened.
1847.	Jan.	12.	Eastern Counties (Ely to Peterborough, $28\frac{1}{4}$ m.) opened.
	Feb.	10.	Wymondham to Dereham (12 m.) opened.
	,,	23.	Lancaster & Carlisle opened with double line.
	Mar.	20.	Whitehaven Junction (12 m.) opened.
	Apl.	20.	Kendal & Windermere opened.
	May	10.	Croydon & Epsom opened.
	,,	24.	Dundee & Perth ($20\frac{1}{4}$ m.) opened.
	,,	28.	Eastern Counties, March to Wisbech, opened.
	Jun.	2.	Southampton to Dorchester opened.
	,,	14.	Havant & Portsmouth opened.
	Jul.	2.	South Eastern (Deal Branch, $8\frac{3}{4}$ m.) opened.
	,,	4.	Whitby & Pickering opened.
	,,	31.	Lowestoft Branch opened.
	Aug.	16.	Narboro' to Swaffham ($5\frac{3}{4}$ m.) opened.
	,,	23.	Gravesend & Rochester reopened.
	,,	27.	Eastern Counties, Cambridge to St. Ives opened.

1847	Aug.	28.	Edinburgh & Glasgow, Shieldhill Branch, opened.
(*continued*)	Sep.	5.	Eastern Union, Hadleigh Branch, opened.
	,,	6.	Erewash Valley (12¾ m.) opened.
	,,	7.	Leeds & Bradford, Skipton Branch, opened.
	,,	18.	Trent Valley opened.
	,,	20.	Edinburgh & Northern opened to Cupar.
	Oct.	2.	London & Brighton, Keymer Branch, opened.
	,,	26.	East Anglian, Downham to Ely, opened.
	,,	31.	Gloucester & Cheltenham Branch opened.
	Dec.	8.	London & Brighton, Newhaven Branch, opened.
	,,	19.	Reading & Hungerford Branch opened.
1848.	Feb.	8.	Watlington to Wisbech opened.
	,,	13.	Weybridge to Chertsey opened.
	,.	19.	Caledonian from Carlisle to Edinburgh opened throughout.
	Mar.	3.	York & Newcastle (Bedale Branch) opened.
	,,	19.	Eastern Counties (Woolwich Branch) opened.
	,,	30.	St. Ives to March (17¾ m.) opened.
	Apl.	3.	Wakefield, Pontefract & Goole opened.
	,,	7.	Melton to Peterborough (26 m.) opened.
	May	5.	South Devon (21¼ m.) opened.
	,,	29.	L. & N.W. Dunstable Branch opened.
	,,	30.	Castle Cary to Perth (45½ m.) opened.
	Jun.	19.	East Lancashire, Blackburn to Accrington, opened.
	Jul.	5.	Edinburgh & Glasgow, Campsie Branch, opened.
	,,	11.	Waterloo Bridge Extn., S.W. Rly., opened.
	,,	24.	Liverpool, Crosby & Southport opened.
	Aug.	1.	Chester & Holyhead opened throughout.
	,,	17.	East Lancashire, Stubbins to Accrington, opened.
	,.	22.	South Western (Richmond to Datchet Branch) opened.
	Sep.	4.	Edinburgh & North (70 m.) opened.
	,,	11.	East Anglian, Swaffham to Dereham (12 m.) opened.
	Oct.	19.	Great Northern, loop line opened.
	,,	29.	Reading to Basingstoke (G.W.R.) opened.
	Nov.	7.	Liverpool & Bury opened to Wigan.

NOTICE TO THE PUBLIC.

The Time Tables forming this little Work are arranged as a Sheet, and published, with the assistance of the Railway Companies, on the 1st of every Month, price 3d. Parties desirous of keeping the Companion correct may be enabled to do so, by purchasing one of those Sheets and substituting the Tables, in which alterations are made, for those in the Work.

The names of such Tables as have undergone a change will be mentioned at the foot of the Sheet

At that time the *Companion* had about fifty pages, so a considerable amount of pasting became necessary, not only by parties desirous of keeping the *Companion* correct, but also by the publishers and agents who wished to keep their old stock up to date.

An attempt at simplification was made in 1842 by printing the Cab Fares and similar information in the ordinary way and stitching the pages together at the end of the book, the maps were then grouped next to the Cab Fares.

By 1844 Bradshaw had discovered that the great British Public is not very good at buying a threepenny sheet of time tables every month, cutting them out and pasting them over the out-of-date tables in a book. So, in that year the Notice to the Public ceased, and in 1845 the *Companion* was published monthly and Bradshaw continued to advertise it for sale until February, 1849.

Robert Louis Stevenson's *Travelling Companion* was returned by a publisher because it was "a work of genius but indecent"; *Bradshaw's Railway Companion* ceased publication because, like so many works of genius, it was not so simple to produce as the Guide which superseded it.

BRADSHAW'S
RAILWAY GUIDE;

CONTAINING

A CORRECT ACCOUNT OF THE HOURS OF ARRIVAL AND DEPARTURE
OF THE TRAINS ON EVERY RAILWAY IN GREAT BRITAIN;

A MAP OF ENGLAND,

WITH THE RAILWAYS COMPLETED AND IN PROGRESS,

HACKNEY COACH FARES, &c.

FOR DECEMBER, 1841.

MANCHESTER:

PRINTED & PUBLISHED BY BRADSHAW & BLACKLOCK, 27, BROWN-ST.

AND SOLD BY

W. J. ADAMS, 170, FLEET STREET, LONDON,

AND MAY BE HAD THROUGH ALL BOOKSELLERS AND NEWSMEN.

Title page of first Guide,
1841

No. 200. $\mathfrak{Entered}$ at $\mathfrak{Stationers'}$ $\mathfrak{Hall.}$ *Price* 6*d.*

3rd *Mo.* (*MARCH*) 1st, 1850.

By Official Authority.

BRADSHAW'S

GENERAL

MONTHLY) RAILWAY AND STEAM NAVIGATION

GUIDE,

FOR GREAT BRITAIN AND IRELAND,

CONTAINING

OFFICIAL TABLES, CAREFULLY REVISED, OF THE HOURS OF DEPARTURE, ARRIVAL, DISTANCE
AND DURATION OF TRANSIT, OF THE TRAINS ON EVERY RAILWAY THROUGHOUT
THE UNITED KINGDOM;

A MONTHLY ALMANACK AND TIDE TABLE;

ALPHABETICAL LIST OF THE STEAMERS,

&c., &c.,

THEIR TIMES OF SAILING FROM EVERY STATION THROUGHOUT ENGLAND, SCOTLAND,
WALES, AND IRELAND, TO HOME AND FOREIGN PORTS, &c.;

THE SAILINGS OF HER MAJESTY'S MAIL PACKETS,

(*Following the Almanack, for which see Contents,*)

PUBLISHED OFFICIALLY IN THIS WORK, BY AUTHORITY OF

THE LORDS OF THE ADMIRALTY;

WITH AN

IDISPENSABLE VARIETY OF MERCANTILE & GENERAL INFORMATION,

ILLUSTRATED BY A SPLENDIDLY EXECUTED

TRAVELLING MAP OF THE RAILWAYS

Of Great Britain and Part of Ireland,

Showing such Lines as have the **ELECTRIC TELEGRAPH** *now in operation.*

HEAD OFFICES OF PUBLICATION.

$\mathfrak{London}$:

W. J. ADAMS, 59, FLEET STREET;
MANCHESTER:—BRADSHAW AND BLACKLOCK, 47, BROWN STREET;
LIVERPOOL:—T. FAIRBROTHER, 2, OLD HALL STREET;
LEEDS:—JOSEPH ASHTON, 96, COBOURG STREET;
EDINBURGH:—HUGH NOBLE, 26, WATERLOO PLACE;
GLASGOW:—R. CHADDERTON, 124, QUEEN STREET (nearly opposite the Royal Exchange);
DUBLIN:—JAMES Mc GLASHAN, 21, D'OLIER STREET;
BRUSSELS:—W. MIDDLETON, 92, MONTAGNE DE LA COUR.

And Sold by all Booksellers and Railway Companies throughout the United Kingdom.

CHAPTER IV

THE GUIDE OF GUIDES

Many humorists have come to grief in attempts to define the most useless thing in the world. Samuel Butler, taking the question seriously, said it was "the last six inches of a line of railway; there is no part of the road so ugly, so little travelled over, or so useless generally, but it is the end at any rate of a very long thing." Then there are those who say it is "last month's Bradshaw" and perhaps it is the truth underlying this destructive witticism ,that accounts for the fact that no copy of Bradshaw's original time sheet appears to have survived, and only one copy of the first number of Bradshaw's Railway Guide. This appeared in December, 1841, and is in the form from which the present Guide has developed. Some of the credit for its publication is said to be due to W. J. Adams, who realised that the *Companion* was a bit too bijou for practical purposes, and its gummy method of production too cumbersome for a regular monthly issue. As a matter of fact, the time tables themselves were printed from the same forms in each case. But instead of being printed on one side of the paper, and cut out and folded and gummed together, as in the case of the *Companion,* those for the Guide were printed on each side of the paper and produced in the same way as an ordinary book, with the result that each page of the Guide was twice the size of those of the *Companion.*

But the great trouble in producing a monthly Guide was obliging the Railway Companies to date their alterations *from* the first of the month, and to furnish their particulars in time for publication *on* the first of the month. A lot of nonsense has been written on this problem which took sixty years to settle.

In the first place it should be remembered Railways were in their infancy, so was the electric telegraph, and there was no such thing as universal time. For instance, in May, 1839, the London and Birmingham Directors ordered that the Time Tables be calculated at the highest rate of speed of the trains between station and station to ensure their not being detained on their arrival from being before time. On June 20th, 1840, they resolved that in the opinion of this Committee, the new Time Tables should be prepared upon the experience of the actual working of the trains—always keeping in mind that the public required each train to perform the journey in the least possible time, with reference to its loading and connection with other lines.

In June, 1844, the Liverpool and Manchester Railway decided to petition Parliament for universal time to be adopted; in October, 1847, the Midland Railway recommended each Company to adopt Greenwich time at all stations as soon as the General Post Office permitted; while the London and Birmingham, on the 14th September, 1838, ordered that the Regulator at the Euston Station be kept to Post Office time and the Regulator at the Birmingham Station to the mean true time at Birmingham. That the Station Clocks on this line be also kept to the mean true time of each station, and that the trains be directed to start three minutes later than the appointed times.

Those readers who can understand the foregoing resolutions will appreciate that in the bad old days the lot of the time table clerk was no sinecure. But what did Bradshaw care? Singleness of purpose, that sounds so noble in an obituary, is a less lovely thing when encountered during the hero's lifetime. True to his Guide, and trustful in the gods, he brushed aside bewildering detail, and on May 12th, 1841, he wrote to the London and Birmingham Company proposing that in future alterations in the times of departure of trains should take place on the first of the month only. By a most suspicious coincidence a letter of the same date appeared in the *Railway Times* of May 22nd:

Railway Time Tables.

To the Editor of the *Railway Times.*

Sir,—I observe that the Directors of the Croydon Railway have advertised in their last notice that they will make no alteration in future in the times of starting their trains except on the *first day of the month.* Now I cannot help thinking that this arrangement would conduce greatly to the convenience of the public if it were universally adopted on all railways. Then if all notices were dated, a passenger would be sure to know whether he had got the last notice in his hand, and a greater degree of usefulness would be given to two excellent publications which I have lately seen, "Bradshaw's Time Table" and "Gadsby's Railway Companion," each published monthly at 3d., and containing the times of starting of all railways.

I am, Sir, your obedient servant,

A RAILWAY TRAVELLER.

May 12, 1841.

Seeing that the Croydon Railway were quarrelling with neighbours at each end of their 8¾m. line, and that a year later they proposed abandoning the working of it and relying on tolls paid by other Companies, this brave resolution may have been no more than a bid for popular favour, especially if they made no alterations in their time tables. The really interesting facts announced by Railway Traveller are that 3d. Bradshaw Time Sheets were in existence on the 12th May, 1841, and that Gadsby's Railway List, which cost 2d. in 1840 when it was started, had become a Threepenny Companion.

Apparently the letter to the London and Birmingham Railway was allowed to lie on the table, for in October, 1846, Bradshaw, who had by that time started the *Railway Gazette*, returned to the subject:

> We may, however, be permitted to make an observation on another part of the subject in which the public are deeply interested. We allude to the frequent necessity which exists of making additions and alterations to the Guide during each current month, in consequence of the later period at which directors arrange their monthly changes of trains. Doubtless this is a point requiring serious consideration, the smaller companies being often compelled to alter their hours of arrival and departure solely on account of changes made by more important lines; but it appears to us that a great part of the inconvenience might be avoided were directors to meet a week earlier than they do at present, and thus permit the Guide to be perfected and published without fail on the first day of every month. Indeed, the Guide will never have attained its full value to the public until each next ensuing number is in the hands of the traveller before the dates of the previous information shall have expired.

Entered at Stationers' Hall.

No. 289.] **8th Mo. (AUGUST), 1857.** [Price 6d. Post Free, 8d.

PUBLISHED OFFICIALLY  EVERY MONTH,

Under the Patronage of HER MAJESTY THE QUEEN
The Royal Family, Both Houses of Parliament, the Government and Public
Offices, &c.,

BRADSHAW'S

GENERAL RAILWAY AND STEAM NAVIGATION

GUIDE,

FOR GREAT BRITAIN AND IRELAND,

CONTAINING

The Authentic Time and Fare Tables of every Railway now Opened for Traffic (the Duration of Transit, &c.), throughout

ENGLAND, WALES, SCOTLAND, AND IRELAND;

To Facilitate Reference, see KEY to the Guide, at page 1.

ILLUSTRATED WITH A COMPREHENSIVE

TRAVELLING MAP OF THE RAILWAYS

OF GREAT BRITAIN, AND PART OF IRELAND,
Shewing the Lines of Navigation, Distances, &c.; The Lines of the Electric Telegraph, &c.

A GENERAL STEAM PACKET DIRECTORY,
ALPHABETICALLY ARRANGED, GIVING THE

DAILY OFFICIAL SAILINGS OF ALL THE STEAM VESSELS DURING THE MONTH
TO AND FROM EVERY PORT AND STATION THROUGHOUT THE UNITED KINGDOM.

HER MAJESTY'S MAIL PACKETS,
PUBLISHED OFFICIALLY IN THIS GUIDE BY ORDER OF THE LORDS OF THE ADMIRALTY;

WITH A LARGE VARIETY OF

LOCAL & VALUABLE INFORMATION COLLECTED COMPILED & ARRANGED EXCLUSIVELY FOR THIS PUBLICATION.

LONDON:—W. J. ADAMS, 59, FLEET STREET, E.C.;
MANCHESTER :—BRADSHAW AND BLACKLOCK, 47, BROWN STREET;
LIVERPOOL :—T. FAIRBROTHER, 46, Dale Street;
BIRMINGHAM :—JAMES GUEST, 52, Bull Street; SHEFFIELD :—ROBERT CHADDERTON, 21, Change Alley;
EDINBURGH :—MOODIE & LOTHIAN, 76, Prince Street; GLASGOW :—JAMES REID, 144, Argyle Street;
DUBLIN : A. CARSON, 51, Grafton Street, (Corner of Stephen's Green);
PARIS :—A. W. GALIGNANI & Co.'s Reading Room, Library, &c., 224, Rue de Rivoli ; J. DAWES, 3, Place Vendome;
L. N. BELLENGER, 212, Rue de Rivoli.
BRUSSELS :—Mr. FLATTAU, Bookseller, Montagne de la Code,
UNITED STATES :—EDWARDS, SANDFORD, & Co., New York, Baltimore and Philadelphia.
And Sold by all Booksellers and at all Railway Stations throughout Great Britain, Ireland, and the Continent.

By that time there were about fifty Companies to co-ordinate, and the problem was not so easy to settle as Mr. Bradshaw seemed to think.

With the increase in the number of Companies an increase had also taken place in the size of the Guide, and while the Guide increased in size, the title page increased in length. The title of the first number of the Guide of December, 1841, was:

BRADSHAW'S

RAILWAY GUIDE;

containing

A correct account of the hours of arrival and departure

of the trains on every Railway in Great Britain,

A MAP OF ENGLAND,

with the Railways completed and in Progress,

Hackney Coach Fares, &c.

No. 2 of January, 1842, contained thirty-two pages, and with No. 7 of June, 1842, the name was changed to Bradshaw's Monthly Railway and Steam Navigation Guide, and by August, 1857—with No. 289—the title page had grown to over 300 words. No. 40 was dated March, 1845, and looking around for something else to increase, the publishers improved the serial number by the addition of 100, so that the issue for April, 1845, was numbered 141.

No. 146, for September, 1845, ran to eighty-nine pages and included a map, with projected lines coloured red, four pages of Continental Time Tables; a table of distances from London to Continental towns; a list of Railways open on the Continent; Places of Amusement, etc., in the Metropolis, Residences of Foreign Ambassadors, Cab Fares from Euston, Paddington and London Bridge, *and* Notices to Correspondents. These last disclose an interesting and almost unbelievable state of affairs:

> The arrangements of the Grand Junction and Liverpool and Manchester Railways, now amalgamated, will undergo considerable changes on the 15th proximo. We can give no information of the arrival of the Manchester and Liverpool trains. Should the united Company publish the information, we shall not fail immediately to adopt it.

In 1830, when all the world was young, the Liverpool and Manchester Directors were wise not to advertise the times of their trains' arrival and made a virtue of necessity, but to have preserved their virtue half way through the roaring forties is a fine, if not the earliest, example of the conservatism of British Railway Administration.

Bradshaw's Correspondents probably saved Kay, the editor, from going mad. From the stuffy atmosphere of dead accuracy in compiling the time tables, he burst into a nipping and an eager air when making his replies:

> *D.W.* is in error, and not the Guide—the train which he supposes to be an *arrival* at Hull is a *departure*.

The date of D.W.'s fall was 1847. About this time Bradshaw was becoming a national institution, for the next year the Comic Bradshaw appeared, a sixpenny brochure by Mr. Angus B. Reach. The contents, which can be adequately described by the words Braw, Raw and Pawky, do not cry aloud for quotation. A quotation from the Lyceum Pantomime for the same year, 1848, runs:

> Luck's a lord, and may provide
> A special train, not marked in Bradshaw's Guide.

Again, in 1851, *The Prince* informed the Lyceum audience:

> My train—despair !
> I can't find anywhere !
> I sooner might in Bradshaw light
> On a train I wanted there !

Both the above masterpieces were by James Robinson Planché, who doubtless had additional qualifications for being appointed Rouge Croix Pursuivant of Arms in 1854, and Somerset Herald in 1866.

Planché's contemporary, Robert Reece, in a Queer Story, introduces the same " aid to Bedlam " theme:

> Almost as useless (howsoe'er you tried
> To follow it) as any Bradshaw's Guide.

But there was a less auspicious recognition that Bradshaw had arrived. Certain printers and publishers approached the Companies offering to print their Time Tables and sell them at -/1d. if the Companies would cease the gratuitous circulation of their own Bills. The result in some cases was that the Companies ceased gratuitous circulation and sold their own time tables at -/1d. But Bradshaw survived; he also survived an episode which is simply told in the minutes of the London and North Western Railway Company of September 10th, 1847:

> The Manager submitted a case of fraud at Wolverton on the part of the Newsvendor who had been selling Bradshaw's Guide of September 1846 for 1847—the year being carefully erased. Read Mr. Curtis's explanation of the manner in which this had taken place, being, as he stated, the result of accident and not intentional. The Committee was not satisfied with Mr. Curtis's explanation and directed the Manager to make further enquiries.

Accidents, of course, will happen, and accidents of this nature were in vogue at the time, for on the back of the Guide for the same month appears:

IMPORTANT INFORMATION.

> Unprincipled individuals, for the sake of gaining a trifle more profit, vend the most spurious compounds under the same names, some under the implied sanction of Royalty and the Government Departments, with similar attempts at deception, while they copy the labels, advertisements, and testimonials (substituting fictitious names and addresses for the real) of the original preparations.

This was from an advertisement of a specific known to Lord Byron, and judging by other advertisements of that time the travellers of 1847 were a C. 3 lot suffering from desperate remedies in addition to desperate diseases.

A complaint of a different sort was mentioned in 1860 by a certain Mr. Smith who remarked on the difficulty of finding in Bradshaw the London and North Western communication with Huddersfield, and that other Companies took especial care to show, in a prominent manner, their route to or from competitive towns.

Something drastic must have been done about Huddersfield, for in 1865 Punch devoted a lot of space to a Guide to Bradshaw. The humour was of the sort described by one of the first contributors to *Punch* in the lines:

> When that old joke was new
> It was not hard to joke.

But *Nemo omnibus horis charivari*, and at a much later date *Punch* wrote:

> The literature of the world contains no book the merit of which is so equally distributed as this masterly work of Bradshaw's. With most books it is possible to point to one chapter that is better than another, or one that is worse. Some books have their best wine at the beginning; some their best at the close. Others again have it in the middle. But Bradshaw is above fluctuation. He rides high, like the stars.

Before coming to that conclusion, *Punch* had one or two outbreaks in his former strain, and in the eighties there was a recrudescence of the complaint against the Railway Companies for not supplying the publishers with notices of changes in time for publication on the first of each month. The hare this time was started by a member of the Royal Archæological Institute. This gentleman, unaware of the jump in the serial number from 40 to 141 in the spring of 1845, was moved to a hopeful protest by the disappointment of a Royal Duke:

> To the Editor of *The Times*.
>
> Sir,
>
> A correspondent informs us that "Bradshaw's Railway Guide" completed its 50th year of publication on the 1st of the present month.
>
> Is it too much to hope that the beginning of its second half-century may be marked with some much needed improvements? These are:
>
> 1. An earlier issue. The inconvenience experienced by those who have to travel on the 1st or 2nd of a new month, from the impossibility of obtaining information of changes in

the time bills, is only too familiar. Why should it be impracticable to issue the new "Guide" a day or two before the end of the current month? This is done on the Continent. Can it not be done in England? It is a simple fact that, the first of July falling on Sunday, it was impossible on Monday to obtain a "Bradshaw" of the present month at either of the railway stations or stationery shops in the city of Lincoln—truly an ill-omened beginning of its second half-century.

2. The complete separation of the market trains, running only once or twice a week, from the ordinary trains. Nothing is more productive of mistake and disappointment than the present confusion of daily and weekly trains on the same page. A burnt bishop was said by Sidney Smith to be the only cure for locked-up railway carriages. One hoped a disappointed Royal Duke might have remedied this unhappy muddle. But the Duke of Edinburgh, during his tour of inspection of the Lincolnshire Coastguard Stations a little while since, fell into the trap, and had to waste some valuable hours at a forlorn little station, and the public were none the better. The Sunday trains do appear in a division by themselves. Why cannot the same plan be adopted for the market trains? A difference of type would make the distinction still more obvious.

3. The publication of the fares. When one has to arrange for a journey for a child, or a servant, or a poor pensioner from one part of England to another, it would be a great convenience to be able to calculate the cost beforehand. This is now impossible, save by correspondence with stationmasters.

We owe much to "Bradshaw." It is compact, well arranged, and, with a little trouble to master its details, very easy of comprehension. The improvements I have suggested would add much to its general utility, and could not be difficult of execution.

Yours, &c.,

EDMUND VENABLES.

The Preceptory, Lincoln.

To the Editor of *The Times.*

Sir,

The letter from the Rev. Edmund Venables referring to our Railway Guide, in *The Times* of the 11th inst., seems to call for some reply.

With regard to the desirability of an earlier issue of the book, we are entirely at one with Canon Venables, and we need scarcely add that our efforts are unceasing to attain this end. We regret, however, that these endeavours are constantly frustrated from causes which, though entirely removed from our own control, we are satisfied might to a large extent be obviated if long-needed reforms in the arrangements of the various railway companies in the alteration of their train services could be secured.

The bulk of the changes effected from time to time by which the publication is delayed are proposed at meetings or conferences of the officers of the various companies, and have afterwards to receive the sanction of the directors. The first essential for the attainment of the desired object is, that these meetings should take place sufficiently early to allow of the *final* settlement of the alterations in time for us to receive and deal with the information, so as to enable us to issue the Guide at least two days before the end of each month. This has been frequently pressed upon the attention of the railway companies, and though we must acknowledge that efforts in this direction have been made in isolated instances, yet for want of combined and mutual recognition of the importance of the subject on the part of the companies generally, they have not as yet resulted in any appreciable improvement.

As will be readily understood, the constantly increasing interchange of traffic arrangements between the different lines tends to add to their complexity, involving a larger expenditure of time in their settlement, so that the difficulty is likely to increase year by year.

We have no hesitation in saying that if a few of the leading companies could realise the importance of the subject and determine that, in the interests of their individual lines, and also of the travelling public—which must necessarily be identical—the ever-recurring and constantly increasing difficulties should be fairly faced, the whole matter could be effectually grappled with.

That it is by no means impossible of attainment is proved from the fact that one of the principal lines furnishes the information, almost invariably, at as early a date as can be reasonably expected.

How essential it is that some step should be taken may be seen from the fact that although, as Canon Venables states, the Guides for July were not obtainable in many districts till the 2nd and 3rd of the month, we have received, since going to press, further alterations from several of the leading lines.

No complaint is more common than the impossibility of settling in advance the details of a journey, with any degree of accuracy, during the closing and opening days of the month, and it is to obviate this that we urge the importance of our proposal.

We have, however, pointed out the one way in which this very desirable end can be obtained, and we can only add that any efforts which may be made will secure our hearty co-operation.

With regard to the minor suggestions of the letter of Canon Venables, which have all claimed our notice for many years past, they are so largely dependent upon the success of what we now propose, that at present they do not come within the scope of practical consideration.

Yours, &c.,

HENRY BLACKLOCK & CO.,
Proprietors of " Bradshaw's Railway Guide."

106, Albert Square, Manchester.

Letters had previously been sent to Joseph Chamberlain, then President of the Board of Trade, on the same subject, and in 1889 and 1901 the question was considered by the Companies—there were a good many of them by then. Finally in 1902 the Companies agreed amongst themselves that:

> Arrangements be made so as to enable the issue of Bradshaw's Railway Guide to take place one week before the first day of the month of its operation.

> Alterations requiring the consent of other Companies to be agreed prior to the 24th of the month next but one previous to their coming into operation.

> Extracts for correction to be sent out not later than the 24th of the month next but one previous, and returned not later than the 1st of the month previous to their coming into operation.

> Information to be forwarded to the publishers of Bradshaw so as to be in the hands of the publishers on the 15th of the month preceding issue. If the 15th falls on a Sunday the information to reach Bradshaw's office on the 14th.

It was no more than reasonable that the time tables should be supplied to Bradshaw in time for publication on the 1st of each month, but it must be borne in mind that where Bradshaw had merely to assemble the information, the Railway Companies had to compile it. An alteration in the running of one main line train may result in scores of alterations to trains running in connection with it, and it was and still is a great achievement on the part of the Railway Companies to have their time tables ready so many weeks in advance. It is fortunate the arrangement was come to, for since it was made great changes have taken place, not only in the volume but also in the nature of passenger services.

Up to 1914 every train was shown in the pages of the Guide, but, since the war, a different type of traffic has developed, and this has resulted in consequent changes in the make-up of Bradshaw. Formerly there was a certain uniformity in the train services, and the Companies' seasonal changes could be anticipated. This is not the case to-day. The great increase in Saturday and Week-end traffic, due to special facilities offered to the public, and the electrification of many of the suburban and coast lines have brought about many changes; and the increase in London Suburban traffic and London Passenger Transport Board services would, if shown in detail in Bradshaw, mean the addition of almost 1,000 pages.

Some idea of the work this would entail may be gathered when it is realised that the average weight of type-setting metal per printed page is 7 lbs. and that for one page alone 250 inches of rule, cut in varying lengths, are required. Five different type faces and four sets of figures are used for each page. This means that approximately 450 characters have to be available for each type-setter.

The Bradshaw pages are compiled from proof copies of time bills issued by the Railway Companies, the alterations in the Guide being carried out in purple ink on special quarto-sized pages printed in green. The compilation of an average single page service is a matter of several hours, the length of time being dependent on the number of connections. A complicated page with intricate connections will occupy a compiler's time for a whole day, and a main line service extending over several pages, a full week for each direction. Even when the compilation of a service is completed a general survey of each page is necessary. Space has to be provided or evenly distributed, all notes, trains and connections accounted for, both on the Companies' time table and on Bradshaw pages, which are then passed to the compositors for correction in type.

A new or heavily altered table is set on a "Monotype" composing machine, but if the alterations are light the standing page is corrected by hand in the composing department. The page is then returned to the compilers for revision from the original copy, and any errors that may be revealed pen-marked on the new proof, which is then recompiled from the Final or Press copies of the Railway Companies' time tables. This second compilation is

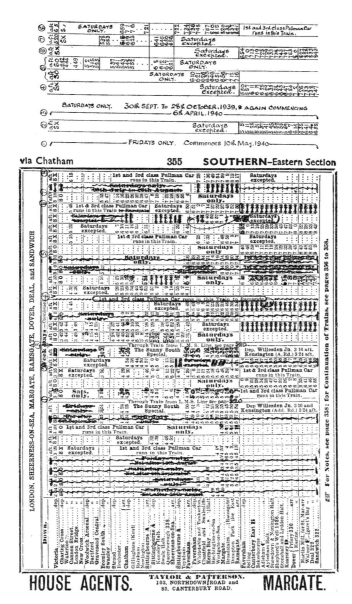

Specimen page of modern Guide, with pen alteration for Printers

once more handed to the case department for correction, and again is returned to the compilers for revision. At each stage of compiling and revising the proof becomes cleaner and the compilers are then able to pass the pages to the case department in batches of 32's for making-up into sheets or sections which are further subject to a final revision before being sent to press.

The Railway Companies' time tables operate for a period of several months, and after being printed and published soon become out of date on account of subsequent changes in the services; the alterations during this period are published by the Companies in monthly Train Alteration Notices issued to Bradshaw for insertion in the ensuing edition.

The introduction of the Summer services creates an addition of over 100 pages, necessitating alterations in the pagination and of the many cross references to be found in the train and station columns, also in the Other Trains notices usually shown in the notes or last page of the service. Heavy alterations in consequence occur in the index, where the most important towns are extensively sub-indexed; this again means further corrections.

The map must be a nightmare to the man responsible for it. Any change in the notation of the tables, any alteration in station names, has to be recorded on it and, when lines have been closed, the relative numbers deleted.

The classified index to the advertisement pages is subject to a monthly revision. The Contents page, the Steamer Information with its own index, and the *House Agents'* page are also dealt with for each issue. Finally, the cover must be dated and numbered—very carefully numbered—it jumped 100 once.

It seems a pity after all that fuss and bother that the book should be out of date in a month. For the man in the train has no time for last month's Bradshaw, unless it be to settle a point of importance in a refreshment room altercation. There is nothing more useless in the world than last

month's Bradshaw unless it be this month's Bradshaw during a coal strike.
Punch discovered that:

Many, I ween, the strike hit hard,
    But none were hurt so much as he,
The soothsayer, the mystic bard,
    Boder of destiny.

Stop ! As he idly penned the word,
    Little he dreamed how more than true
His statement was. The engines heard,
    Stop ! And they did stop too.

Saturdays only ! How serene,
    With what wise calm he used that phrase,
And now there is no 9.15,
    Sundays or Saturdays.

And so with all the wiles he planned
    Large output of laborious brains,
The asterisks, the little hand
    That points to *Other Trains*.

Vain little hand ! Enough, enough;
    I will not see page 94;
Pathetic fragment of a cuff,
    Thou canst not aid me more.

But fallen is the pride of those
    Who knew their Bradshaw, Perth to Tring;
And jubilant are Bradshaw's foes,
    Who blessed the blooming thing.

And he himself—a poor wan ghost—
    I see him on some ancient loop,
The trickiest piece he loved the most,
    His own dumbfounded dupe;

At Basingstoke I see him, too,
    Sitting on some deserted seat,
Or Blisworth Junction, watching through-
    Connections fail to meet.

Waiting alone, but ah ! for what ?
    As the dull leaden hours roll by,
' I hear her—no, I hear her not,
    Forsaken—Bradshaw—I ! '

110   For Continental Railway Information,
See Bradshaw's Continental Railway Guide for March.

COACHES

, In connexion with Trains on the Leamington Branch, see page 40.

ALTERATION OF TRAINS on and after December 1st, 1849.

The SHAKESPEAR Omnibus, between LEAMINGTON and ALCESTER, through Wellesbourne, Stratford-on-Avon, and Red Hill.——On and after the above date, the Shakespear Omnibus will leave the Globe Inn, Alcester, every Morning, except Sunday, at 9 o'clock, meeting Trains at Leamington Station, which arrive in London at 5 30 p.m. and in Birmingham at 1 40 p.m., waiting arrival of the Train which leaves London at 12 noon, and arrives back at the Globe Inn, Alcester, at 8 o'clock.

FARES:—Leamington and Stratford-on-Avon......Inside, 3s.; Outside, 2s. 0d.
Leamington and Alcester ....Inside, 6s.; Outside, 3s. 6d.
Bath and Regent Coach and Railway Offices, Leamington.   [1-3-50—W.B.

In connexion with Trains on the North Branch, London & North Western Railway,
Pages 35 and 36.

Between WHITMORE STATION and SHREWSBURY, through Market Drayton, Hodnet, and Shawbury,
The Victoria continues to run as usual from the George Inn, Shrewsbury, every morning (except Sundays)
at 7, meeting at Whitmore the up train at 11 10 and the down train at 11 50 a.m., and arriving in Chester
at 1 35, Manchester at 1 50, Liverpool at 2 15, Birmingham at 1 35, and London at 7 p.m.; waits the
arrival of the up train at 1 38 p.m., leaving London at 6¼, Birmingham at 10, Liverpool at 11¼, Manchester
at 11 40, and Chester at 11 50 a.m., and arrives back at the George Inn, Shrewsbury, at 5½ p.m.

[R-3-50—W.D.G.

TRAVELLING TO NORTH WALES, &c. &c.
THE OLDEN TIME REVIVED.

THAT FIRST-RATE APPOINTED FOUR-HORSE COACH,

THE DEFIANCE,

CONTINUES TO RUN DAILY (SUNDAYS EXCEPTED) TO DOLGELLY.

THE "DEFIANCE" leaves the Llangollen Road Station, on the Shrewsbury and Chester Railway, at a quarter to Twelve o'clock, a.m., after the arrival of the 10 40 train from Chester, and 10 15 a.m. from Shrewsbury, passing through the beautiful Vale of Llangollen, Corwen, Bala, &c., &c.; it also leaves the "Ship Hotel, Dolgelly" daily (Sundays excepted), at a quarter to Ten o'clock a.m., for the Llangollen Road Station, arriving in time for the express trains to Shrewsbury, Birmingham, and London; also to Liverpool, Manchester, and all parts of the North.

CHARLES CASTLE takes this opportunity of most sincerely thanking his Friends and the Public for the support given to his Coach, and begs to assure them of his continued exertions to merit their patronage.

Persons desirous of travelling by this Coach, should leave by the following trains, viz.: Birmingham at Eight o'clock, Wolverhampton at half-past Eight o'clock, Manchester at a quarter to Nine o'clock, Liverpool at half-past Nine o'clock, Shrewsbury at a quarter past Ten o'clock, and Chester at twenty minutes to Eleven o'clock.

☞ Passengers booked at the Llangollen Road Station, and Ship Hotel, Dolgelly.

CHARLES CASTLE, Proprietor.

Bradshaw's Guide March 1850

London Views—from Tourist Handbook,
1866

CHAPTER V

INSULAR AND CONTINENTAL

Of all the early General Railway Time Tables, Bradshaw alone has survived, and of all the early periodicals devoted to Railways the *Railway Gazette*, started by Bradshaw, is the only name that continues at the present time.

The first number of *Bradshaw's Railway Gazette* appeared on Saturday morning, July 12th, 1845, and announced:

BRADSHAW'S RAILWAY GUIDES SENT FREE BY POST.—The Proprietors of Bradshaw's Railway Guides and other Railway and Steam Navigation Tables, inform the Public that arrangements are in progress for printing a portion of their Time Tables, &c., &c., on Stamped Paper, to pass Free by Post, as a newspaper ; which arrangements, they make no doubt, will prove satisfactory to their subscribers. They hope to have the arrangement complete in time for their next monthly issue ; when their Tables, which have often been characterised as the Railway Traveller's indispensable companion, may be sent Free, to any part of the United Kingdom.

To be had of the Publishers in London and Manchester ; at the various Railway Stations ; and through any Bookseller or Newsvender.

N.B.—In ordering these works, please to describe them as under :—

BRADSHAW'S THREEPENNY RAILWAY GUIDE—THE SHEET.

BRADSHAW'S THREEPENNY RAILWAY GUIDE—THE BOOK.

BRADSHAW'S SIXPENNY RAILWAY AND STEAM NAVIGATION GUIDE,—

This contains a list of the Steam Packets to and from the various Ports in the United Kingdom.

BRADSHAW'S RAILWAY COMPANION,

Price 1s., (containing numerous Railway Maps and Plans of Towns,) will be published as usual, but not stamped.

The Stamped Editions will be charged 1d. extra ; and may be had at Bradshaw's Railway Publication Office, 59, Fleet-street, London, or 27, Brown-street, Manchester.

In the second number, July 19th, two more notices appeared:

BRADSHAW'S RAILWAY MAPS.

I.

In the press, and will be published immediately, By GEORGE BRADSHAW, Assoc. Inst., C.E.,

A NEW RAILWAY MAP of ENGLAND and PART of SCOTLAND, on which will be accurately laid down, by the respective Engineers of each line, all the Railways Completed, in course of Formation, or Projected, up to the present time. In addition to the general Railway Information which this Map will contain, it will be a most Accurate and Valuable Map of the Country, on which all the Roads, Canals, and Rivers, will be correctly laid down. The size of the Map will be four feet by three feet.

Price in Sheets, Coloured...................... £0 12 6
Ditto in Case 0 18 6
Ditto Mounted on Rollers and Varnished...... 1 9 0

II.

Shortly will be published, By GEORGE BRADSHAW, Assoc. Inst., C.E.,

A NEW RAILWAY MAP of FRANCE, All the Railways, both Projected and Completed, up to the present time. Printed upon one large sheet, forty inches by twenty-four inches.

Price, in Sheets...................... 3s. 0d.
Ditto Ditto, Coloured...................... 4s. 6d.
Coloured and Mounted .... 10s. 0d.

Independent of the Railway Information which this Map will contain, it will be an excellent Map of the Country, on which all the principal places will be accurately laid down.

Sold by Bradshaw and Blacklock, 27, Brown-street, Manchester, and 59, Fleet-street, London.

To show how broad-minded Bradshaw was, he suffered an advertisement to appear in the third number stating "a list will be forwarded to any part of the Kingdom on the receipt of *a Queen's head*."

Every week in his Gazette Bradshaw published Addenda to Bradshaw's Railway Guide, giving particulars of any alterations in train services made since the previous week, and every week the new map was announced to be " in preparation." The Map of France was ready in September, and the second edition of the Map of Great Britain in November. Bradshaw thought highly of this map, and said so in his Gazette:

> Bradshaw's Second Edition of his New Map of the Railways of Great Britain.—London and Manchester.
>
> The high encomiums bestowed on the first issue of this splendid production have only served to stimulate a higher degree of enterprise in the projector. The map now before us, we hesitate not to say, is unmatched in England for boldness of conception, accuracy of delineation, and richness of colouring. Taken from the Ordnance Survey, it contains the fullest and most accurate geographical information extant, and shows the course of all our railways through every town and village of note in the kingdom. The sections form a highly valuable appendage, showing, as they do, the gradients on the principal lines, and thus form a ready school for instruction, or authority for reference, to all interested in the progress and construction of railways. This gorgeous map is on the same scale as that intended for presentation to our readers, and is only superior to it in the display of the sections and the high tone of colouring given to the counties and lines of railway by careful and skilful artists.

So after all the Guide was only a medium for selling maps.

In the number for November 8th, 1845, Bradshaw advertised a real collector's piece: ˙

> Bradshaw's Railway and Steam Navigation Guide.
> In consequence of some slight alteration in the Time Tables of the Great Western, the South Eastern, the Greenwich, the Bolton and Leigh, and the Preston and Wyre Railways, since

the early issue of this publication, a Supplement has been issued, containing the corrected Tables, which will be delivered gratis to such persons who may have purchased the early Edition, on application to the Office, 59, Fleet Street, or to their respective Booksellers or Newsmen.

Volume IV, No. 103, for Saturday morning, November 28th, 1846, contained a brief notice:

To our Readers.

The property of The Gazette having changed hands, the Editor begs most respectfully to announce that his connexion with it ceases from this day. London, Nov. 28, 1846.

With the 104th issue of December 5th, 1846, the name was shortened to The Railway Gazette, and in the place where once the name of Bradshaw reigned the Royal Arms appeared. The Gazette continued to be printed and published by Wm. Jas. Adams until December 12th, 1846, and on and after December 19th by Alexander Laidlaw, of No. 4, Flood's Terrace, Walworth.

But the Gazette was not the first nor the last of Bradshaw's periodicals other than time tables.

On the 1st May, 1841, price -/1½d., appeared Bradshaw's Manchester Journal, embellished with Maps and Engravings in Steel and Wood. On November 6th the name was changed to *Bradshaw's Journal*, and it was published weekly until December, 1842, and then monthly until May, 1843. It was also embellished with poetry.

Some time in 1842, while the maps were still enriching the Manchester Journal, W. J. Adams, the London Agent, seems to have moved from 170 to 59, Fleet Street, and here he employed Edward Litt Leman Blanchard, who fifty years later was described as the Santa Claus of pantomime at Drury Lane, who often referred with pleasure to the time when he was employed as one of the compilers of the now celebrated Bradshaw's Guide.

Apparently Mr. Blanchard's pleasure took the form of saying that:

The Railway Companies were at first vehemently opposed to the scheme, and in their niggard way refused to supply their tables on the ground that it would make punctuality a sort of obligation, and that failure would bring penalties. G. Bradshaw however was not to be repulsed, and by various devices, notably by taking many shares, brought over the hostile Companies.

This is a favourite passage for quotation by writers on Bradshaw, some of whom suggest Blanchard was a Railway Director. As a matter of fact he was the son of a celebrated actor and was first employed in the Dramatic Department of the Daily Telegraph, and he was the reputed author of Bradshaw's Descriptive Railway Guide, Adams' Illustrated Descriptive Guide to the Watering-Places of England & Companion to the Coast; Adams' Illustrated Guide to the English Lakes, Adams' Descriptive Guide to the Environs of the Metropolis; The Stranger's & Visitor's Conductor through London; and Adams' Descriptive Guide to the Channel Islands, the Isle of Wight, and the Isle of Man, etc.

In 1846 Adams published Bradshaw's Descriptive Guide to the South Eastern Railway, and Guides to Tunbridge Wells; Maidstone; Ashford; Canterbury; Folkestone; Dover; Ramsgate; Margate; etc., together with their Historical and Local Associations, by E. L. Blanchard; and Bradshaw's Descriptive Guide to the Great Western Railway, Part II, from Bristol to Plymouth, "containing everything of importance to the Railway Tourist, and forming a Complete Traveller's Companion to each Town and Station along the line and the attractive scenery adjacent," by E. L. Blanchard.

About 1850 was published Bradshaw's Handbook to the Manufacturing Districts of Great Britain, "furnishing a very instructive detail of the various branches of art carried on in the Counties of Lancaster, Chester, Stafford, and Warwick, by E. L. B., illustrated with well-executed county maps." Maps again ! Those were the days of long and communicative titles, and they were the days of the Baxter print for which Bradshaw became a licensee. He sent for Frederick Shields and asked him, Dost thee think thyself able to design for Baxter's patent oil-printing process ? Shields thought he was able and was offered 10/- a week as designer. Shortly afterwards, in 1851, the year of the Great Exhibition, Bradshaw's Guide Through London and its Environs was published. It contained a coloured frontispiece of nine small views. In the centre was a view of the Exhibition surrounded by

MANCHESTER TO NORMANTON	Week Days.											Sundays.			
	1 & 3 gov.	2 & 3 gov.	3 & 2	4 & 2 mail.	5 & 2	6 & 2	7 & 2	8 & 2	9 & 2	1 & 2	10 & 2	1 & 3 gov.	2 & 3 ml.gv.	3 gov.	4 gov.
	morn.	morn.	morn.	morn.	aft.	aft.	aft.	aft.	aft.		aft.	morn.	morn.	aft.	aft.
MANCHESTER......dep.	...	6 0	8 15	10 15	12 10	1 30	3 5	5 5	5 40		7 40	8 0	10 15	5 0	7 30
Miles Platting	...	6 8	...	10 21	...	1 35	3 11	...	...		7 46	8 6	10 21	5 6	7 36
Middleton	...	6 21	8 25	10 32	...	1 45	3 21	5 15	...		8 1	8 19	10 32	5 16	7 49
Blue Pits	...	6 33	8 35	10 40	12 28	1 54	3 32	...	6 0		8 13	8 32	10 40	5 25	8 0
ROCHDALE	...	6 41	8 40	10 50	12 35	2 0	3 40	5 31	6 7		8 20	8 39	10 50	5 33	8 10
Littleborough	...	6 45	...	10 57	...	2 7	3 47	5 38	...		8 28	8 47	10 57	5 40	8 19
Walsden	7 0	...	...	...	...	2 17	3 58	5 49	...		8 40	9 0	...	5 53	8 33
TODMORDEN	5 30	7 5	8 53	11 0	12 53	2 22	4 5	5 52	6 23		8 45	9 6	11 9	5 58	8 38
Eastwood	5 36	7 13	...	11 19	...	2 28	4 10	5 56	...		8 53	9 10	...	6 3	8 43
Hebden Bridge	5 42	7 21	9 0	11 19	...	2 34	4 18	6 3	6 32		9 0	9 15	11 19	6 10	8 51
Mytholmroyd	5 46	7 25	...	...	...	2 38	4 22	...	...		9 5	9 20	...	6 14	8 55
Luddenden Foot	5 50	7 29	...	11 28	...	2 42	4 26	...	...		9 10	9 26	11 28	6 18	9 0
Sowerby Bridge	6 0	7 38	9 13	11 33	1 15	2 50	4 36	6 10	6 40		9 20	9 32	11 33	6 27	9 8
HALIFAX......dep.	6 0	7 45	9 0	11 28	1 5	2 40	4 26	...	6 30		9 10	9 25	11 25	6 18	9 0
North Dean	6 6	7 45	...	...	...	2 56	4 43	...	...		9 28	9 39	...	6 35	9 15
Elland	6 10	7 50	9 20	...	...	2 59	4 47	...	6 47		9 32	9 45	...	6 39	9 20
Brighouse	6 16	7 58	9 25	11 50	1 27	3 6	4 56	...	6 52		9 41	9 52	11 50	6 48	9 28
Cooper Bridge	6 20	8 4	...	...	...	3 11	5 0	...	...		9 46	10 1	...	6 54	9 36
Mirfield	6 35	8 15	9 35	12 0	1 38	3 22	5 14	...	7 8		10 0	10 3	12 0	6 59	9 45
Dewsbury	6 45	8 26	...	12 10	...	3 32	5 26	...	7 16		10 10	10 13	12 16	7 6	10 0
Horbury	7 0	8 35	...	12 21	...	3 42	5 34	...	...		10 10	10 19	12 22	7 18	10 0
WAKEFIELD	7 15	8 45	9 53	12 30	1 57	3 52	5 42	...	7 26		10 28	10 31	12 30	7 2	10 18
NORMANTON	7 25	8 55	10 0	12 40	2 5	4 0	5 50	...	7 35		10 40	10 41	12 40	7 3	10 30

No 1 down Train runs to Knottingley meet Great Northern Train

Page from Lancashire and Yorkshire Railway Time Tables, 1852

eight tiny views of the Thames, Buckingham Palace, and other famous buildings, each measuring about 1in. by 1½ins.

This Guide is another collector's piece, as in addition to containing Bradshaw's first Baxter print, four well-known men were associated with it, Bradshaw, Baxter, Blanchard and Shields. For Shields, who began at 10/– a week, became an associate of the Royal Institute of Painters in Water Colours; the friend of Rossetti and Ford Madox Brown; and the decorator of the Duke of Westminster's Chapel at Eaton Hall. His most remarkable work is still to be seen by those Londoners who visit the Chapel of the Ascension in Hyde Park Place.

The following year, 1852, Bradshaw and Blacklock printed the working time tables for the Lancashire & Yorkshire Railway, but the Railway Company decided to transfer the printing of this to Messrs. Grant & Company, Manchester, possibly to save money, for they could not have been more beautifully printed than in Bradshaw's large clear type.

Another publication of that period published by Bradshaw & Blacklock was Samuel Salt's Statistics and Calculations, essentially necessary to persons connected with Railways or Canals, containing a variety of information not to be found elsewhere. The title of this book of Samuel was quite correct in one particular of "information not to be found elsewhere." It was Mr. Salt's habit to season essential statistics with wise saws and ancient instances, and his calculations alternated with such pleasant surprises as:

"What should one read for ? For ! Why, to know facts.—Pope."

"Knowledge is proud that he has learned so much; Wisdom is humble that he knows no more.—Cowper."

"To a man full of questions make no answer.—Plato."

and more surprising still,

"No man can faithfully serve two masters.—*Salt.*"

But it is impossible to enumerate all the publications that have issued from the house of Bradshaw & Blacklock. In 1858 two pages of the Guide

BRADSHAW'S ILLUSTRATED HAND-BOOK OF FRANCE, Illustrated with splendid Travelling Map of France, Plan of the Principal Cities, and numerous well-executed Steel Engravings of the Chief Places of Resort in France. Elegantly bound in Turkey Red, Price 5s.
"The most convenient comprehensive Travellers' Hand-book for France hitherto published."—Vide French Press.

BRADSHAW'S COMPANION TO THE CONTINENT. By E. L. Blanchard, Esq. A Descriptive Hand-Book to the Chief Places of Resort, their Characteristic Features, Climates, Scenery, and Remedial Resources; with Observations on the Influence of Climate and Travelling. Price 7s. 6d., cloth.

BRADSHAW'S ILLUSTRATED GUIDE THROUGH LONDON AND ITS ENVIRONS, giving, in a new and comprehensive form, all that can be seen in the British Metropolis, and its Vicinity for thirty miles round. Illustrated with Oil-Coloured Prints, Wood and Steel Engravings, and beautiful Maps of London and its Environs for thirty miles round. Price 3s. 6d., cloth.

BRADSHAW'S GUIDE TO THE NEW CRYSTAL PALACE AT SYDENHAM, with Map and Exterior View of the Palace and Grounds, Park, &c. Price 6d.

BRADSHAW'S HAND-BOOK TO THE MANUFACTURING DISTRICTS OF GREAT BRITAIN; furnishing a very instructive detail of the various branches of Trade of Lancashire, Cheshire, Staffordshire, and Warwickshire; with well-executed Maps and Engravings. Price 3s. 6d., cloth.

BRADSHAW'S GUIDE THROUGH EDINBURGH, with Illustrations. Price 1s.

BRADSHAW'S SHAREHOLDERS' GUIDE AND RAILWAY MANUAL FOR 1857, with Maps of the Railways—British and Continental. Price 7s. 6d., bound in cloth, embossed and lettered.

BRADSHAW'S RAILWAY ITINERARY AND GENERAL CONVEYANCE GUIDE TO EVERY TOWN, VILLAGE, AND PARISH IN GREAT BRITAIN, FOR 1857; giving the Mode of Access, Mileage, &c., from the Metropolis; the nearest Railway Station, and distance therefrom to the adjacent towns, &c., &c.; to which is added a list of all the Railway Stations, where situated, the Route therefrom, and the various Companies' Lines by which to travel; also a complete Electric Telegraph Directory and Map of the Railways of Great Britain, the whole giving full and correct information, in a form and by means of Vertical and Horizontal Lines. Price 2s. 6d.; Cloth, 4s. Post Free, 2s. 3d. and 4s. 2d.

BRADSHAW'S RAILWAY MAP OF GREAT BRITAIN (Size, 6 feet 3 inches by 5 feet 1 inch), exhibiting, at one view, all the Railways, Railway Junctions, &c., with their Stations, the Lines of the Electric Telegraph, the Canals, Navigable Rivers, and the Mineral Districts, with their Geological distinctions clearly marked, defined from the latest and most approved authorities, reduced from the Ordnance Survey. Mahogany Rollers, Varnished, £4 4s.; Library Case, £4 4s.; Sheets, Coloured, £1 1s.

BRADSHAW AND BLACKLOCK'S Copy Slips, Atlases, Maps, and the Shilling Volumes of their POCKET LIBRARY, their Improved and beautiful selection of Oil-Coloured Prints (Baxter's Process), always on sale at BRADSHAW'S RAILWAY GUIDE OFFICE (W. J. Adams), 59, Fleet Street, London, and at their Establishment, 47, Brown Street, Manchester.

TO TOURISTS AND COMMERCIAL TRAVELLERS

BRADSHAW'S PUBLICATIONS

ARE TO BE HAD AT EVERY

RAILWAY STATION, BOOKING OFFICE, AND BOOKSELLER'S THROUGHOUT THE UNITED KINGDOM, AND THE PRINCIPAL CITIES OF THE

CONTINENTS OF EUROPE AND AMERICA, INDIA AND AUSTRALIA.

BRADSHAW'S MONTHLY RAILWAY AND STEAM NAVIGATION GUIDE OF GREAT BRITAIN AND IRELAND, with splendid Map of Great Britain, with all the Railways and Lines of Navigation. Price 6d.
Published monthly.

BRADSHAW'S THREEPENNY GUIDE for all the Railways, with Map. Published monthly.

BRADSHAW'S CONTINENTAL RAILWAY, STEAM NAVIGATION, AND GENERAL CONVEYANCE GUIDE OF EUROPE, including every useful and practical information for Visitors to all parts of the Continent, with splendid Map of Northern and Central Europe. Price 1s. 6d. Published monthly.

BRADSHAW'S CONTINENTAL RAILWAY GUIDE AND GENERAL HAND BOOK, giving, in addition to the Railway and Steam Information, a Descriptive Guide to the most frequented parts of the Continent, including the Overland Route to India, Guides to Turkey, Algeria, &c. Illustrated with clear Travelling Maps of EUROPE, also Maps of France, Belgium, Switzerland, Panoramic Maps of the Rhine, and Plans of Paris, Lyons, Marseilles, Brussels, Antwerp, Ghent, Mayence, The Hague, Ostend, Cologne, Frankfort-on-the-Maine, Berlin, Hamburg, Munich, and Dresden. Price 3s. 6d., bound in cloth, with pockets, &c. Published monthly.

NEW EDITIONS.

BRADSHAW'S GUIDE THROUGH PARIS AND ITS ENVIRONS, with a new and beautiful Steel-Engraved Plan of the French Metropolis and Environs, exhibiting, in a novel and comprehensive form, all that can be seen, and how to see it, with the least fatigue, time, and expense, forming a complete and indispensable Companion to the Visitor to Paris. Price 2s. 6d., cloth.
This excellent Hand-Book to the French Metropolis has been most promptly translated by the British, Continental, and American Press as a most meritorious production, whether it be regarded for the full, clear, and judicious compilation, or the unsurpassed cheapness—embracing, as it does, not only all that can be seen within this beautiful City and its Environs, but also for the comprehensive instructions it imparts to every Parisian Visitor. Every line of Bradshaw's Paris Guide is not only useful, but really valuable information—the general remarks for Travellers particularly so; the Illustrations are positively Works of Art, and the Maps are in every respect worthy of the world-wide fame of Bradshaw. The lowness of the price places it within the reach of every class of visitors; indeed, the purchase of this Guide Book will greatly tend to economise the expenses of a TRIP to PARIS.

BRADSHAW'S ILLUSTRATED HAND-BOOK FOR BELGIUM AND THE RHINE, AND THROUGH RHENISH PRUSSIA, with numerous Engravings, illustrative of the Scenery and Architecture, Natural Beauties of Belgium and the Rhine, with splendid Steel-Engraved Travelling Maps, and Town Plans of the Various Cities, &c. Elegantly and conveniently bound in Turkey Red, Price 6s

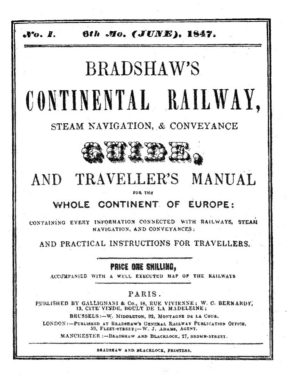

Fac-simile (reduced) of title-page of the first "Continental" Bradshaw,
1847

were filled with advertisements of them, which included Bradshaw's
Continental Railway Guide and General Handbook. By 1914 this last had
developed into a marvellous combination of Time Table, Baedeker, and
Hotel Guide. It was first published in June, 1847, and appeared monthly
until August, 1914. But the Great War put an end to all that, and a copy
of No. 807, which some people regard as the last of the Continental Bradshaws,

has realized as much as £5. On some occasions it may have been worth more to some people—Corney Grain, for instance, composed a song by stringing together the names of certain Italian stations; and once when Bertram Mills was in search of a first class equine act he heard that the famous Orlando troupe was performing at a small town 20 miles from Stockholm. He flew to Stockholm and hired a car. After travelling about forty miles he began to get alarmed, but fortunately he thought of looking in his Continental Bradshaw and there found reassurance in the statement that 20 Swedish miles equal 125 English miles.

The English Bradshaw has been put to similarly exotic uses. Nat Gould, who appeared to write not only four out of every five of the yellow backs once to be seen on the bookstalls, and invented a title racy of the turf for each, used to name his characters from the Index to Bradshaw's Guide. "Miles Platting and Newton Heath," he used to say, "sound quite nicely, and they don't sue you for libel, however unpleasant they turn out." And in 1903, when a well-known weekly paper offered "£5 a week for life" as a prize in a competition in which competitors had to guess the names of stations from pictorial puzzles, the demand for Bradshaw's Guide increased threefold, with the result that the Index was issued separately at 3d.

The Continental Guide now appears in a modified form of about 620 pages, and is as indispensable as Bradshaw's International Air Guide which made its appearance in November, 1934. At present the Air Guide runs to less than 250 pages, so a larger type and stouter paper can be used which make it the most perfect of all time tables.

Two other publications of Bradshaw ranked second only to the Guide. The Shareholders' Manual, first issued in 1848 and published annually until 1923, covered the whole constitutional history of all the British Railways, and in addition published each year the Railway & Canal Commission and Board of Trade Reports, and gave also particulars of Traffic Agreements between Companies, Reports of Committees of Investigation and Royal Commissions; reviewed Railway legislation, and contained Bradshaw's one and only joke. Like all Railway jokes it was perennial. For many years under the heading *Arbroath and Forfar Company* it solemnly announced

Cover of first International Air Guide,
1934

" Two Directors rotate in order required by Act every year "—apparently for joy at being re-elected. It is a pity that the Arbroath and Forfar Company was dissolved by the Railways Act, 1921, which was passed with a view to the reorganisation and more efficient working of the railway system of Great Britain.

A curious mistake occurred in the serial numbering of the Manual. Apparently somebody deducted 1848 from 1857 and finding the answer 9, called the 1857 issue Volume No. IX, whereas it was the tenth. The mistake persisted to the end, the last volume being designated "seventy-fifth edition." The first edition of 1848 had an article on The Electric Telegraph and Uniformity of Time. It began:

> Thou wondrous, whispering wire !
> Thou time and space-annihilating wand !
> Thy marvels are beyond
> All thought to which our intellect may aspire.

However, intellect did its best for about five closely printed pages, and towards the end explained that " in Manchester, on the 1st of February, the sun rises at 7h. 34m. and sets at 4h. 26m. by the sun; but his time of rising by the clock is 7h. 48m., and he sets at 4h. 40m." This rather suggests that where Intellect ends Superstition begins, and Bradshaw, while refusing to give the Sun a Capital S at the outset, thought he had better address him as a gentleman in the latter half of the sentence. The symbol "No. 1" had already been appropriated for January.

The second number of the Manual advertised "on the first of each month, price Twopence, Bradshaw's Metropolitan Railway Guide Sheet showing at one view the daily communication between the Metropolis and the Principal Towns in Great Britain, with the Times of Departure from and Arrival at the different London stations plainly laid down in an entirely new and simplified plan." This may have been a sheet form of Bradshaw's London and Conveyance Guide which appeared in November, 1848. From the advertisement in the Manual it looks as though Bradshaw had anticipated the A.B.C. Guide, which appeared in October, 1853, and was certainly the forerunner of Bradshaw's London Railway Guide which, starting in December, 1862, price 0/4d., continued for nine months. It reappeared in December, 1867, and in September, 1868, it became the London & Provincial Bradshaw, and finally disappeared in 1887.

But Bradshaw's Manual is best described in the Publisher's Address for 1853:

It unfolds at once the whole of that complicated machinery in Railway economy, a full development of which is of such vast importance to the Railway community; and completely annihilates every thing which can operate as a barrier to a perfect knowledge of the system upon which it treats.

The same might truthfully be said of Bradshaw's Canals and Navigable Rivers of England and Wales, a thirty-shilling volume and cheap at the price. It contains the sentence, "Gunpowder boats have to leg through;" declares that "The largest wherry ever built was the Wonder of Norwich," and gives the meaning of Chalico, Gongoozler, Henhouse Rangers and Josher. A most readable book.

However, all good things must come to an end, and it only remains for me to make one personal acknowledgment. I should indeed be ungrateful if I were to close this talk without mentioning one name, without whose book I might indeed have been a lost man; one whose advice, invariably correct, was expressed in the most condensed, not to say epigrammatic, form; always correcting my train of thought, never prepared to compromise with my desires. When I have doubted what course to follow, it is to his pages that I have turned, and never turned in vain. Often when I have wondered where I would find tomorrow's dinner, he has relieved my anxiety; and by following his advice I have not gone hungry. Amid the bustle and clatter I have slept soundly, through having first sought his aid; and even those of his pages which are devoted to advertisement have sometimes helped to find a pillow for my head. I refer, of course, to MR. BRADSHAW.

That must be true. It was "on the wireless," and they are not allowed to advertise. Apparently they have to be impersonal as well, or Mr. Maurice Healy, who gave the talk, would assuredly have referred to the editor of the Guide, Mr. C. Way, and to his predecessors, Mr. W. T. Knight, who succeeded Mr. Kay in 1880, and Mr. F. S. Walton who followed Mr. Knight in 1903 until Mr. Way took charge in 1932.

CHAPTER VI

CHANGING TIMES

Vic Bradshaw-Mitchell

George Bradshaw married Martha Darbyshire on 16th May 1839 and they had two sons. Both joined Bradshaw & Blacklock; Christopher was the elder and died on 27th April 1928. William had died on 26th January 1926 in his 81st year.

The term Bradshaw continues in use in the name of the national railway timetable of India and in Australia it was applied to two different publications in the 1860s.

The Grouping in 1923 involved the merging of around 100 railway companies into the "Big Four". This had an impact on Henry Blacklock & Co., and three of the four slowly decided to use the relevant section of Bradshaw as their official timetable.

The Great Western Railway was the only company not to have had its name changed in 1923 and was the only one to maintain its own timetable production.

The Southern Railway was the first to offer a section of Bradshaw as its public timetable, this starting in 1924. Its trains were entirely green and so this colour was used on the cover of the publication.

The London Midland & Scottish Railway followed this example, but with its characteristic dark shade of red. The London & North Eastern Railway adopted the system shortly before the advent of World War II in September 1939. This left the GWR and it succumbed with the advent of emergency timetables on 25th September 1939. A volume was issued on 23rd October 1939 with the title *Bradshaw's Guide to the British Railways*. It had a substantial market as travel by road was very limited, due to severe petrol rationing. *Bradshaw's Continental Railway Guide* ceased for good in 1939.

Paper rationing at the commencement of the war presented a multitude of problems, but Bradshaw was deemed essential and there is no evidence of reduction in production. However, the The History of Bradshaw was delayed

No. 1372.] **12th Mo. (DECEMBER), 1947.** **[Price, 1/- net.**

BY APPOINTMENT
PUBLISHERS OF BRADSHAW'S GUIDES
TO HIS MAJESTY THE KING
HENRY BLACKLOCK & CO LTD., PROPRIETORS & PUBLISHERS OF

BRADSHAW'S
OF**F**ICIAL GUIDE EVERY MONTH
FOR GREAT BRITAIN AND IRELAND
Containing the Official Time Tables, specially arranged, of all Railways.

✱✱ The Tables in this book are compiled with as much care as circumstances will
✱ permit; but it must be distinctly understood that the Proprietors do not hold
themselves in any way responsible for inaccuracies. It will be esteemed a favour
if early intimation be given of any error that may be found in the Guide.

LONDON:—HENRY BLACKLOCK & Co. LTD., PROPRIETORS AND PUBLISHERS, BRADSHAW HOUSE,
5, SURREY ST., STRAND, W.C.2.
Telephone—TEMple Bar 2842-3-4. 'Grams—"Bradshaw, London."
MANCHESTER;—HENRY BLACKLOCK & Co. LTD., EDITORIAL DEPT., ALBERT SQUARE, 2.
Telephone—BLAckfriars 4218 (2 lines). 'Grams—"Guide, Manchester."
DUBLIN:—EASON & SON LTD., 50, MIDDLE ABBEY STREET (Sole Agents for Bradshaw's Publications in Ireland).
[Rtd. at Stationers' Hall.

CONTENTS.

LONDON'S BRIGHTEST BOOKSHOP
Come to TRUSLOVE & HANSON, 14a, CLIFFORD STREET, W.I.
THE BOOKSHOP off BOND STREET

Contents list for the last Bradshaw's Guide
issued prior to railway nationalisation.

having been planned for publication in October 1939. The date of release was not printed on it; maybe the paper fell off the back of a lorry, as was common in those difficult days. (Your scribe was welcomed as a volunteer van boy, as the tarpaulin-covered lorries had no rear doors.)

Paper quality suffered and various coloured hairs could be seen in many of the fascinating pages.

Advertising was reduced, with hotels taking 52 Bradshaw pages in 1940 and only 42 in 1943. Holidays were largely a thing of the past and most of the few remaining posters on stations were headed "Is your journey really necessary?". Others ordered only 4ins of bath water, as every possible economy had to be made.

Bradshaw lost the advertisements from its covers and spine, but internally there were a few. Some told you where you could make your Will or obtain "a haven of quiet". South Coast and East Coast residents had to move away or remain in their dwellings when the invasion started, so Bradshaw came in useful again.

Special trains run during the war numbered 9.3m for troops and 0.58m for prisoners. Over 0.4m wounded men were conveyed. Bradshaw was of value to the 0.62m service personnel travelling on ordinary trains, although often indirectly. They usually received journey details from staff at their camp before starting and there were also special offices at the major stations, where advice could be obtained. Bradshaw was again of assistance here.

After the war ended in 1945, Bradshaw's austere exterior, free of advertisements, continued throughout the long period of national austerity. Rationing prevailed: food, fuel, furniture, clothing and much else, but not fish. Paper was still limited, but Bradshaw received its ration satisfactorily. The thickness of *The Railway Magazine* was 1¾ins in 1939, but was limited to ½ins from 1942 until 1949. Bradshaw was steady at 1½ins from 1940 to 1945, but had returned to a healthy 2ins by 1947.

Paper shortages generated an inconvenient problem in the convenience. Many people had to resort to the Victorian practice of cutting up newspapers, making a hole through the corner of a wadge of squares and threading string through it. A retired Bradshaw was ideal, as it only needed a loop of string, near the middle page.

The GWR took the shortage seriously and demanded that station masters returned all the wooden rollers from the holders to the stores at Swindon, recording the transaction with a delivery note. Presumably Bradshaws were used in 1st class waiting room toilets, where an interesting read could be had while waiting. The bottom line is "Bradshaw to the rescue again".

The different British Railways regions moved to larger pages ($9\frac{1}{4}$ x 6ins) in the early 1950s and went to other printers. Bradshaws were produced this size from 13th June 1955 and were 2ins thick initially, this rising to a maximum of almost 3ins.

Railway preservation began with the Talyllyn Railway in 1951, but this route had been shown continuously in Bradshaw from the early days. The first restored line was that of the Festiniog Railway, albeit only part of it. A Saturdays-only service, intended for shoppers, was shown in September 1956 running between Portmadoc Harbour and Penrhyn. It was discontinued at the start of 1957, but the Summer trains were shown later that year and the table is included herein. The Bluebell Railway was the only revived standard gauge line to appear in Bradshaw. In 1961 it was the pioneer.

The last issue of Bradshaw appeared in May 1961, but Henry Blacklock & Co. continued to print various BR publications for some time. At the peak, Bradshaw showed 160 different railway companies and over 21,000 miles of routes. The final edition was numbered 1521, but a sequence of 100 numbers was inexplicably unused, in 1845.

CHAPTER VII

INTEREST IN TIMES

Vic Bradshaw-Mitchell

Hereon, the text is written in the first person, as it relates to my railway publishing venture, which started in 1981. But first, a few notes on my interest in timetables. I was making observations of the Shepperton branch trains from my bedroom window at Hampton from my earliest days and was soon noting their timings.

From about the age of ten, most of my spare time (outside air raids) was spent on the nearby station, where life revolved around .09 and .39 departures. I was welcomed into all departments and worked as a volunteer, with the consent of the station master. Regular trips were made to Clapham Junction to observe train movements and timings, not engine numbers.

My interest extended to bus timetables, which I bought by post at 6d each and when 12 years old, I started making trips by bus to our holiday home on the Sussex coast at Selsey. The timings had to be approved by my parents, who went by car, but my routes were very varied, Oxford being one memorable deviation.

I still have my first railway purchase: the LNER issue for 1st October 1945. (My grandparents had returned to live at Clacton-on-Sea by that time). I collected every Southern issue thereafter. When a student, I travelled home on the 5.16 from Waterloo platform 16 and met a young lady who was 16. (In due course we were married and Barbara has typeset all my texts, including this one).

It was while a student at Guy's Hospital Medical School that I first met a Bradshaw and thereafter started collecting them, usually from the rubbish bin. National Service followed so I was then able to visit the bin at RAF St. Athan Officers Mess regularly. They were of value for touring Wales on the two free passes received per annum. My 1961 copy was obtained during a Guy's clinical meeting; it was the last year of issue and a sad time for me.

I was subsequently able to buy one issue for every year back to 1869, except for 1886, 1891 and 1900, which still elude me. Surprisingly, one large batch came from South Africa. Every subsequent BR edition has been carefully stored.

The 25th anniversary of the cessation of passenger trains to my home town of Midhurst took place in 1980 and so I organised an exhibition for church funds. It resulted in the creation of *Branch Lines to Midhurst* with Keith Smith and I developed Middleton Press for its production in 1981.

My Bradshaws were of great value in compiling the PASSENGER SERVICES section of this album and also about 400 others which have followed. One reviewer said that we are "Evolving the Ultimate Rail Encyclopedia". Many Bradshaw extracts are reproduced therein, for the pleasure of all.

→ The final page for the British Isles was no. 1178 in the August 1957 issue and it includes the nation's first revived railway, at the bottom of the page. The Dublin-Cork service was on the facing page and the Irish Republic continued to the last one.

Tables M 3 to M 9a

Table 3 — DOUGLAS, ST. JOHN'S, RAMSEY and PEEL—Isle of Man

EXTRA TRAINS on Sundays (commencing 30th June) to Kirk Braddan departing Douglas at 10 10, 10 40 am. Returning after the Open-air Church Service.

A Not after 18th July.   B Commences 19th July.   ‖ Calls at St. Germain's by request.   † Request stop.

Table 4 — DOUGLAS, CASTLETOWN and PORT ERIN—Isle of Man

D Commences 1st July   † Request Stop.

Table 4a — DOUGLAS, LAXEY and RAMSEY—Manx Electric Railway

Douglas (Derby Castle) to Ramsey (Plaza).   WEEK DAYS and SUNDAYS at 7 0, 8‖50, 10 0, 10†30 and 11 0 am; 12‖0 noon; 1 0, 2 0, 2 30, 3 15, 4 0; 4‡50, 5 30, 6 30, 8‖0, 9 0, and 10‖30 pm. Trains call at Laxey 30 and arr Ramsey (Plaza) 75 minutes after leaving Douglas (Derby Castle)

Ramsey (Plaza) to Douglas (Derby Castle).   WEEK DAYS and SUNDAYS at 6‖45, 8 20, 10‖15, 10†30 and 11 30 am; 12 0 noon; 12 30, 1 45, 2 30, 3 30, 4 0, 4 30, 5 30, 6†30, 7 15, 8 30, 9 30 and 10§30 pm. Trains call at Laxey 40 and arr Douglas (Derby Castle) 75 minutes after leaving Ramsey (Plaza).
‖ From Laxey only.   § 7 30 pm on Sundays.   † Except Sundays.   ‡ To Laxey only on Sundays.   § Except Sundays.   To Laxey only.

Table 5 — RAVENGLASS and DALEGARTH—Ravenglass & Eskdale

a Stops to set down only.   b Stops to take up only.   E Except Saturdays.   S or § Saturdays only.

Table 6 — LLANBERIS and SNOWDON SUMMIT—Snowdon Mountain—5 miles
Runs until 19th October inclusive

Llanberis to Snowdon Summit—Week Days at 10 0 and 11‖0 am; 12 0 noon; 1 30, 2 0, 3 0 and 4‖30 pm
Snowdon Summit to Llanberis—Week Days at 11 30 am; 12‖30, 1 30, 3 0, 3 30, 4 30 and 6‖0 pm
No train will run with less than twenty return passengers, or the equivalent in Adult Fares
Trains will only run weather and other causes permitting
‖ Will not run after 14th September

Table 7 — LIVERPOOL, BIRKENHEAD and ROCK FERRY—Mersey (L.M.R.)

Liverpool (Central Low Level and James Street) to Hamilton Square, Birkenhead Central, Green Lane (Tranmere) and Rock Ferry (Bedford Road). MONDAYS TO FRIDAYS at 6 0, 6‖15, 6 15, 6 25, 6 35, 6 45, 6 50, 6 55, 7 0, 7 5, 7 10, 7 15, 7 25, 7 35, 7 38, 7 45, 7 55 and every 5 minutes until 9 5 am, at 9‖10, 9 15, 9‖20, 9 25, 9‖27, 9 35 am and every 10 minutes until 4‖37, 4 45, 4 54, 5 0 and every 5 minutes until 6 20 pm, 6 35 and every 10 minutes until 7 15 pm, then 7‖18, 7 25 and every 10 minutes until 11 5 pm, then 11 25 and 11‖33 pm. SATURDAYS at 6 0, 6‖15, 6 15, 6 25, 6 45, 6‖50, 6 55, 7 0, 7 5, 7 10, 7 15, 7 25, 7 35, 7 38, 7 45, 7 55 and every 5 minutes until 9 5 am, at 9‖10, 9 15, 9‖20, 9 25, 9‖27, 9 35 am, and every 10 minutes until 1 35 am, at 1‖37, 1 53 am, 12 0 noon and every 5 minutes until 10 51 pm, then 11 25 and 11‖33 pm. SUNDAYS at 7 26, 7 46, 8 21, 8 51 and 8 51 am, and every 15 minutes until 10 56, 11 7, 11‖10 pm and 11 10 pm. Minutes at Stations after leaving Liverpool (Central)—James Street about 2, Hamilton Square 5, Birkenhead (Central) 8, Green Lane 10, Rock Ferry 13.
Rock Ferry (Bedford Road), Green Lane (Tranmere), Birkenhead Central and Hamilton Square to Liverpool (James Street) and Central Low Level. MONDAYS TO FRIDAYS at 5‖45, 5 55, 6 5, 6 15, 6 25, 6 35, 6‖44, 6 45, 6‖52, 6 55, 7 0, 7 5, 7 15, 7 20, 7 25, 7 35, 7 45, 7 50 and every 10 minutes until 9 10 am, at 9 16 am and every 10 minutes until 1 6, 4 50, 4 59, 5‖1, 5 10, 5 25, 5 35, 5‖40, 5‖45, 6 35, 5 45, 5 750, 5‖40, 6 40 and every 5 minutes until 6 10 pm, at 6 20, 6 30, 6 36, and every 10 minutes until 11 6 and 11 13 pm. SATURDAYS at 5‖45, 5 55, 6 5, 6 15, 6 25, 6 35, 6‖44, 6 45, 6‖52, 6 55, 7 0, 7 5, 7 15, 7 20, 7 25, 7 35, 7 45 and every 5 minutes until 11 35, 11 43, 11 50, 11 56 and every 5 minutes until 11 6 and 11 13 pm. SUNDAYS at 7 26, 7 46, 8 21, 8 51 and 8 51 am, and every 15 minutes to 10 51 pm. Minutes at Stations after leaving Rock Ferry—Green Lane about 2, Birkenhead Central 5, Hamilton Square 7, James Street 10, and Central Low Level 12.

A To Birkenhead Central.   B From Birkenhead Central.   § Except Fridays.   Z Fridays only.

Table 9 — SWANSEA and MUMBLES—Mumbles Electric

Frequent Service between Swansea (Rutland Street) and Mumbles Pier Week Days and Sundays, time on journey about 19 minutes, calling at Argyle Street 2, St. Helens 4, Brynmill 6, Ashleigh Rd. 9, Blackpill 11, West Cross 13, Norton Road 14, Oystermouth (Station for Langland Bay and Caswell Bay) 16, Southend 17 and arr Mumbles Pier 19 minutes after leaving Swansea (R. St.).

Table 9a — PORTMADOC (Harbour), MINFFORDD and PENRHYNDEUDRAETH—Festiniog

A Runs 15th July to 7th Sept.   B Tues., Weds., Thurs. and Sats. 16th July to 7th Sept.

All Trains call at Pen Cob, Boston Lodge and Pen-y-Bryn Halts By Request

A typical cover for Bradshaw's Guide in its final year of publication.

CHAPTER VIII

IT'S THAT NAME AGAIN

Vic Bradshaw-Mitchell

The Press announcement in 2007 that the printed timetable would cease shocked me. It was reported that sales had dropped to 14,000, a joyful figure in the eyes of most book publishers.

Many wrote to their MPs about the legality of such a move and it seems the Commons Select Committee for Transport thought otherwise. It presumably ordered The Stationery Office (once "Her Majesty's") to produce it.

In the meantime, a letter was sent to Network Rail to advise that Middleton Press would be willing to publish it. The long journey to their Leeds office was followed by a cool reception, but the offer of the data followed. There was no mention of TSO.

Here was the opportunity to revive the long forgotten name of Bradshaw and so I adopted the pen name shown above, as editor. The pleasure was short lived, as when W.H.Smith was approached regarding sales on the stations, their reply was that they only wanted one timetable and TSO's will do. This was most surprising. Validity date was 9th December 2007.

Having supplied them with thousands of my albums, I was known to have some knowledge of railways, but there was no desire to compare the products. I went to their Waterloo branch, paid for a copy and then found that the map had apparently fallen out. The staff could not find maps in any others and I was told to complain to the publisher. The call resulted in my being told to complain to the retailer and abrupt termination thereof.

This is thought to be the first timetable ever to be devoid of a map and the first to claim UK coverage, when it only dealt with Great Britain. My solution to the map problem had been to segment the Network Rail route diagram onto sequential pages, so that the reader could select the chosen region of interest and see the table numbers.

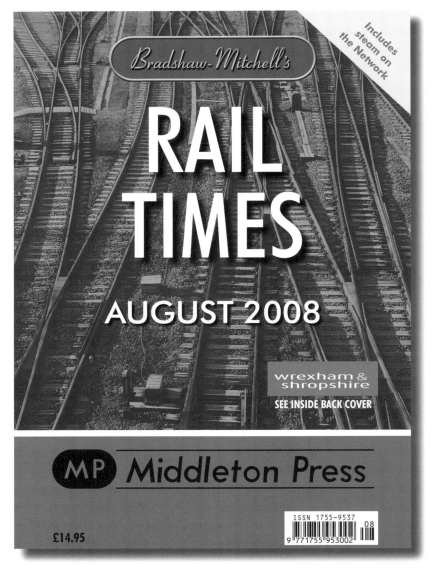

During its period of monthly publication, Middleton Press was able to include timings for a new open access company.

Just as Bradshaw lost 100 numbers, Bradshaw-Mitchell's appeared to lose 10. This was due to monthly production in the first 12 months. A freshly set Eurostar timetable appeared in all Middleton Press products from the outset, but in the other volume that company's widely criticised presentation appears. For apparently the first time in 170 years, the stations were placed across the top of the page, instead of a column on the left! However, this is agreeable to W.H.Smith on behalf of the travelling public and frustration prevails. None of the regular heritage trains on the network have been shown, although a claim is made that all trains are shown.

As a cartographer, Bradshaw would have appreciated two features I have added to recent editions. Inside the front cover is a colour map of Great Britain showing each Train Operating Company, it being provided by Barry Doe, of the journal RAIL. The back cover has a detailed diagram in colour by Andrew Smithers of Project Mapping.

The National Railway Museum opened The Bradshaw Room in 2008 for research purposes and it has an extensive collection of Bradshaw publications. The Bradshaw-Mitchell range is complete.

Network Rail moved from Leeds to new offices in Milton Keynes in 2010, but the timetable staff did not. Further problems followed with inexperienced operators, new computer systems and TOCs which introduce new timetables when it suits them.

Finally in April 2010, a graduate with operating experience was put in charge of timetable publications and the problems were soon greatly reduced. It was Victoria Fox and in December 2011, she put her head above the battlements by inviting readers and travellers to make comments direct to her. It seems that Bradshaw never needed to do so, although he also had trouble with uncooperative railway companies in the early years.

The final frustration to record is that small omissions occurred on the route map, which were easily corrected after I spotted them. The new HS1 service to Maidstone and the new station at Buckshaw Parkway were not included. Costing millions, the TOCs must have been exasperated at the potential loss of revenue from these enterprising additions.

It seems that Middleton Press made history in the railway publishing world in April 2012, by producing ebooks in that field, including this publication. Thus this volume is an unexpected part of Bradshaw's History, which, no doubt, he would have enjoyed.

CONTENTS

EDITORS NOTES

I am glad to greet you in this fourth revision of the timetable for Great Britain by Middleton Press. It gives me pleasure to state that the price rise anticipated in my last notes has not taken place, owing to a greatly increased circulation. My thanks go to everyone who has helped bring this about. However, this may be necessary for the next issue, due to unpredictable changes in these turbulent times.

Alterations at validity date are fewer this year and those with computer access can download amendments for selected tables as follows:

Go to www.google.co.uk
(type in search) network rail current timetable
(select network rail - current timetable)
(scroll down & select) additional alterations

If devoid of a computer or helpful family, friends or neighbours, such print-outs can be obtained at most public libraries. Help can be received by using the telephone number shown on page 5.

Fares can be obtained on line at www.nationalrail.co.uk/passenger_services/manuals.html

Tickets can be obtained by post and times confirmed by using Ffestiniog Travel (01766 512400). In this way you support the survival of this historic and unique railway.

May 2009   Vic Bradshaw-Mitchell

Page 1 of the May 2009 Rail Times reveals the range of contents. A survey showed that 92% of readers did not need a magnifier when there were two tables per page.

CHAPTER IX

BACK TO THE PAST

Vic Bradshaw-Mitchell

Railways have been Britain's biggest hobby for decades, but the BBC has for long ignored this fact. However, a new series began in 2010 titled *Great British Railway Journeys* and all the programmes were introduced by Michael Portillo. The policy was to visit largely interesting businesses dating from the Victorian era, with quotations read from "*Bradshaw's Guide*", so called. In reality, the book shown was four copies of *Bradshaw's Handbook for Railway Tourists*, bound in cloth in 2008. The brief new title chosen was that used for Bradshaw's timetables for 120 years, but this was apparently unknown to the programme makers.

The TV series has been very popular, with visits to many fascinating and unusual premises, mostly not open to the public. The railway journeys are often shown on diagrams to be over routes that have never existed, but the frequent readings from *Bradshaw's Guide* add atmosphere and provide a vivid link with the past.

In its final week in January 2012, the programme was viewed by an average of 2.43 million people, each evening. These peeps at the past have brought that important name to an immense audience.

After much searching, I was able to find four 1866 copies, each with sets of identical advertisements. Middleton Press was able to have the text reprinted, with one set of advertisements and all the maps. The original engravings were scattered and were collected together within a total number of 620 pages. Publication was on 22nd October 2011 and sales rocketed. It was soon in the top six at Amazon and the Middleton Press mail order folk have been busier than ever before.

I rejoice that Mr Portillo has revived this splendid production from the past and that it can be supplied to so many with no previous knowledge of its joys. They can now enjoy *Bradshaw's Rail Times* from different eras and look forward to *Bradshaw's Continental Guide 1913*, which is in preparation.

BBC *Great British Railway Journeys.* SERIES ONE was first broadcast in January 2010, SERIES TWO in February 2011 and SERIES THREE in January 2012.

SERIES ONE

Liverpool to Eccles
Manchester to Bury
Todmordon to York
Pontefract to Bridlington
Filey to Scarborough
Preston to Morecombe
Settle to Garsdale
Windermere to Kendal
Carlisle to Glasgow
Edinburgh to Kirkcaldy
Swindon to Bristol
Yatton to Western Super Mare
Torquay to Totnes
Bugle to Mevagissey
Truro to Penzance
Buxton to Matlock
Cromford to Burton-on-Trent
Walsall to Bournville
Coventry to Watford
St Pancras to Westminster

SERIES TWO

Brighton to Crystal Palace
Waterloo to Canary Wharf
Enfield to Cambridge
Ely to King's Lynn
Dereham to Cromer
Ledbury to Shrewsbury
Telford to Wrexham
Chester to Conwy
Llanwrst to Porthmadog
Llanberis to Holyhead
Newcastle to Chester-le-Street
Durham to Grosmont
York to Saltaire
Batley to Sheffield
Langley Mill to Melton Mowbray
London Bridge to Chatham
Aylesford to Tunbridge Wells
Canterbury to Margate
Sandwich to Folkestone
Hythe to Hastings
Ayr to Paisley
Dumbarton to Tyndrum
Oban to Corrour
Roybridge to Glenfinnan
Lochailort to Skye

SERIES THREE

Great Yarmouth to Beccles
Darsham to Felixstowe
Sudbury to Southend
Epping to Hackney
Fenchurch St. to Embankment
Windsor to Didcot
Reading to Alton
Winchester to Isle of Wight
Brockenhurst to Poole
Wareham to Portland
Oxford to Pershore
Hartlebury to Great Malvern
Lydney to Newport

Cardiff to Brecon
Port Talbot to Milford Haven
Berwick-upon-Tweed to Morpeth
Bardon Mill to Wigton
Cockermouth to Eskdale
Kirkby-in-Furness to Lancaster
Heysham to Snaefell
Bray to Dublin
Enfield to Drogheda
Dundalk to Portadown
Belfast to Whitehead
Ballymoney to Londonderry

ADVERTISEMENTS.

FOR

AIR TRAVEL

Henry Blacklock & Co. Ltd., of London and Manchester, announce that SO SOON AS CIRCUMSTANCES PERMIT they will resume the monthly publication of

BRADSHAW'S
BRITISH & INTERNATIONAL
AIR GUIDE
(FIRST PUBLISHED NOVEMBER, 1934)

Bradshaw's British & International Air Guide will contain all the Air Routes of Great Britain and the British Empire, Europe, Asia, United States of America, South America, North Africa, with Times of Departure and Arrival, Distances, Fares, Foreign Currency, Booking Offices, Maps and Official Route Numbers.

Intending Subscribers should send their names and addresses for registration to the Proprietors, Bradshaw's British & International Air Guide, Bradshaw House, 5, Surrey Street, Strand, London, W.C.2, or instruct their Newsagents to do so.

Ever optimistic, the publishers included this in the January 1945 issue, many months before the war had ended.

MP Middleton Press

★ ALBUM SERIES TITLES ★

Branch Lines	Scottish Main Lines
Narrow Gauge Railways	Country Railway Routes
South Coast Railways	Great Railway Eras
Southern Main Lines	London Suburban Railways
Eastern Main Lines	Welsh Valleys
Western Main Lines	Mineral Railways
Midland Main Lines	Tramway Classics

Leisurely armchair journeys back in time.
Each station is visited in geographical order.
Photographs give a visual history of each location.
Over 400 albums bound in attractive glossy hardback covers.
Recent volumes available as ebooks.

★ BOOKS ★

Specialist Railway Books
Shipping and Waterways
Military Books
Trolleybuses

★ BRADSHAWS ★

Bradshaw's Guide
As seen on TV

Bradshaw's Rail Times Reprints
The classic timetables reissued

Rail Times for Great Britain -
Showing the latest timetables. Issued twice per annum.
Editor Vic Bradshaw-Mitchell

Please request our brochure or visit our website. The latter includes an index
to stations contained in all Middleton Press albums. This now extends to
around 100 pages and is updated regularly.

MP Middleton Press
EVOLVING THE ULTIMATE RAIL ENCYCLOPEDIA

Easebourne Lane, Midhurst,
West Sussex. GU29 9AZ
Tel: 01730 813169 Fax: 01730 812601

Email: info@middletonpress.co.uk www.middletonpress.co.uk